OBAMA'S CHALLENGE

America's Economic Crisis and the Power of a Transformative Presidency

Robert Kuttner

CHELSEA GREEN PUBLISHING
WHITE RIVER JUNCTION, VERMONT

Developmental Editor: Joni Praded
Project Manager: Emily Foote
Copy Editor: Laura Jorstad
Proofreader: Bill Bokermann
Book Designer: Peter Holm

Printed in the United States of America
First printing, September 2008
10 9 8 7 6 5 4 3 2 1   08 09 10 11 12 13

Our Commitment to Green Publishing

Chelsea Green sees publishing as a tool for cultural change and ecological stewardship. We strive to align our book manufacturing practices with our editorial mission and to reduce the impact of our business enterprise in the environment. We print our books and catalogs on chlorine-free recycled paper, using soy-based inks whenever possible. This book may cost slightly more because we use recycled paper, and we hope you'll agree that it's worth it. Chelsea Green is a member of the Green Press Initiative (www.greenpressinitiative.org), a nonprofit coalition of publishers, manufacturers, and authors working to protect the world's endangered forests and conserve natural resources. *Obama's Challenge* was printed on a 30-percent postconsumer-waste recycled paper supplied by BookSurge. This paper is acid and chlorine free and is certified by the Forest Stewardship Council (FSC). The ink used in printing is biodegradable and recycled and contains no lead or toxic chemicals.

Library of Congress Cataloging-in-Publication Data

Kuttner, Robert.
  Obama's challenge : America's economic crisis and the power of a transformative presidency / Robert Kuttner.
    p. cm.
  Includes bibliographical references and index.
  ISBN 978-1-60358-079-3
  1. Financial crises--United States. 2. United States--Economic policy. 3. Political leadership--United States. 4. Obama, Barack I. Title.
  HB3743.K79 2008
  330.973--dc22

                            2008035247

Chelsea Green Publishing Company
Post Office Box 428
White River Junction, VT 05001
(802) 295-6300
www.chelseagreen.com

For Doris Kearns Goodwin

ALSO BY ROBERT KUTTNER

That people can be lifted into their better selves is the secret of transforming leadership . . .

—James MacGregor Burns

Contents

one

A Great President or a Failed One

There is a tide in the affairs of men.
Which, taken at the flood, leads on to fortune;
Omitted, all the voyage of their life
Is bound in shallows and in miseries.

— SHAKESPEARE, *Julius Caesar*

Barack Obama could be the first chief executive since Lyndon Johnson with the potential to be a transformative progressive president. By that I mean a president who profoundly alters American politics and the role of government in American life— one who uses his office to appeal to our best selves to change our economy, society, and democracy for the better. That achievement requires a rendezvous of a critical national moment with rare skills of leadership. There have been perhaps three such presidents since Lincoln.

Obama unmistakably possesses unusual gifts of character and leadership. Because of the deepening economic crisis, he will have to move imaginatively and decisively. He will need all of his inspirational and political skills, as well as ones he is still learning.

On January 20, the recession that he inherits from George W. Bush will become his. He will need to act quickly to prevent further deterioration in what is already the worst financial collapse since the Great Depression. The American economy could return to a path of recovery and shared prosperity—or rapidly spiral downward.

Voters will expect concrete improvements as well as loftier

national aspirations. As a simple matter of politics, if the crisis deepens in 2009 and he fails to deliver relief, his support could well erode and he could lose a working legislative majority midway through his first term in the 2010 elections. Then the country would face economic crisis coupled with political stalemate.

Obama will be challenged both by hard economic realities and by the constraints of conventional wisdom. In principle, two core premises about the economy, which have governed the economic thinking of both major parties for three decades, have been demolished by the deepening crisis. The first is that markets can accurately price complex financial inventions, with no need for government involvement. The second is that private outlays are invariably superior to public ones.

Economic recovery will require the drastic revision of these premises, just as in 1933. The Federal Reserve and the Bush Administration have already engaged in massive bailouts of private financial institutions, seemingly blowing away the idea that markets don't need government. Yet we have a national case of cognitive dissonance, for the same outmoded ideological assumptions linger on. The administration now accepts emergency interventions countermanding the free market—but only in practice, not in theory.

Despite the severe economic situation, there is an undertow of stale thinking that discourages transformative policies. Even with increased Democratic majorities in both houses of Congress and a great deal of goodwill, progress will be far from automatic. The new president will need to inspire the American people to demand enactment of bolder measures than either the Congress or Obama himself currently thinks necessary or possible.

As Doris Kearns Goodwin, to whom this book is dedicated, observes, all of the great presidents used their leadership first to transform the public understanding of national challenges and then to break through impasses made up of congressional blockage, interest-group power, voter cynicism or passivity, and conventional wisdom. In different ways, Abraham Lincoln,

Franklin Roosevelt, and Lyndon Johnson found allies, respectively, in the abolitionist movement, the labor movement, and the civil rights movement, as well as the press and the general public. Each president grew immensely in office. Each changed the national mood, then the direction of national policy.

They did not do so by being "post-partisan," or centrist, but by taking huge political risks on behalf of principles that the people came to deeply respect. Often they enlisted some members of the opposition party in their cause, thereby splitting the opposition—but not by splitting the difference. Yet they also functioned as great unifiers.

By appealing to what was most noble in the American spirit, these presidents energized movements for change, and thereby put pressure on themselves and on the Congress to move far beyond what was deemed conceivable. They generated accelerating momentum for drastic reform that proved politically irresistible. The abolition of slavery seemed beyond possibility in 1860, as did the vastly expanded federal role in the economy in 1932, and the full redemption of civil rights in 1963.

As Goodwin notes,

> History suggests that unless a progressive president is able to mobilize widespread support for significant change in the country at large, it's not enough to have a congressional majority. For example, Bill Clinton had a Democratic majority when he failed to get health reform. When you look at the periods of social change, in each instance the president used leadership not only to get the public involved in understanding what the problems were, but to create a fervent desire to address those problems in a meaningful way.

To the list of transformational presidents we must add one conservative, Ronald Reagan. The achievements of Reagan did not make our economy or society a more attractive habitat for most people, but they nonetheless represented profound change. Americans who were often dubious about what Reagan was selling found themselves liking the man. He had a sunny optimism. After the depressing years of the 1970s, people were ready for "morning in America." Reagan was admired for his willingness to take risks on behalf of principles, however flawed the principles themselves. He had the gift of leadership, and behind Reagan were armies of strategists able to turn a personal triumph into a systematic ideological reversal. Reagan succeeded in transforming public assumptions from the general premise that government should help to the idea that government was likely to make matters worse. Thanks to very effective Republican campaign machinery, ideological zeal, and party unity, that presumption held for another two decades—until it was ultimately discredited by events.

Now it is time for the wheel to turn again. Barack Obama has both the national moment and the raw material to be a transformative president. A forty-six-year-old freshman senator, an African American no less, does not decide to pursue his party's nomination against an all-but-certain presumed nominee unless he has an unerring sense of timing, confidence, and a feel for the bold stroke. Obama has exceptional skill at appealing to our better angels and a fine capacity to be president-as-teacher. He inspires, as only a few presidents have done.

But Obama will need to be a more radical president than he was a presidential candidate. Radical does not mean outside the mainstream. It means perceiving, as a leader, that radical change is necessary, discerning tacit aspirations and unmet needs in the people, and then making that radical change the mainstream view for which the people clamor.

Obama, in his books and speeches, has been almost obsessed with the idea that people are sick of partisan bickering. Yet he also has claimed the identity of a resolute progressive. Can he be both? History suggests that it is possible both to govern as a radical reformer *and* to be a unifier, and thereby move the political center to the left. But that achievement requires wisdom, resolve, and leadership. The easier course is to split the difference, as our last two Democratic presidents have done, and just move to the center generally. This is also what our last two losing Democratic nominees did. Their strategy failed to either inspire liberals, co-opt conservatives, or move enough swing voters. It signaled: *Just another politician.*

Presidential candidates, as they assemble legions of pollsters and campaign consultants, are at grave risk of being turned into risk-averse mush. As this book will explain, this seems to be more of a recent Democratic malady than a Republican one. Lincoln, Roosevelt, and the Lyndon Johnson of the civil rights era needed no polls. They were exquisitely tuned to public opinion, a talent that helped them to be superb tacticians; but each was anchored by a strong inner compass as well. To the extent that Obama relies more on his handlers than on his own core convictions, he weakens his unique self.

Three disclaimers: The alert reader will have noticed that I am making the heroic assumption that Barack Obama will be our next president. It is more than a little presumptuous to publish a book on the eve of an election on the premise that a particular candidate will win. I certainly don't have a crystal ball. But this slightly cheeky exercise enables both writer and reader to raise important questions about the obstacles that Obama will face, the choices he needs to make, and the stuff he is made of.

Second, those who become excited about a particular candidate are at grave risk of getting their hearts broken. There were times when even Roosevelt did things that appalled his most fervent admirers. As a veteran of forty years of close observation of politics, I am not a soft touch. Nor am I working as an adviser or consultant to the Obama campaign, except to the extent that this book can be read as a citizen's open letter. I believe, based on the evidence, that Obama has the capacity to be both a unifier and a transformational progressive. However, I am writing this book not as a cheerleader but as a sober counterweight to a lot of bad advice that he will receive to simply govern as a post-partisan, pragmatic centrist.

And third, in coming months there will be dozens of detailed policy proposals from think tanks and advocacy groups on all the things President Obama needs to do. For the most part, this book is not a manifesto. It is rather an examination of the dynamics of presidential leadership and its capacity to transform public assumptions and expectations, drawing on the achievements of great presidents. While there are some policy proposals herein, one lesson from history is clear. Fine programmatic ideas often fail unless a president succeeds in capturing the public imagination.

Transformational presidents, when they succeed, also transform political alignments. The two emblematic cases of the past century were of course Franklin Roosevelt and Ronald Reagan. The Roosevelt coalition, notwithstanding the Eisenhower interlude, lasted for thirty-six years, from 1932 until 1968. The Reagan coalition, despite Clinton's presidency, lasted for twenty-eight, from 1980 to 2008. Lyndon Johnson was on the way to renewing a durable progressive majority coalition, but his Vietnam debacle short-circuited his domestic achievements and invited a very different realignment. Lincoln could well have produced a constructive realignment, had he lived to serve out a second term, "with malice toward none and charity for all." But in the event, the Republicans who succeeded him began by brutally punishing the white South, then proceeded to abort Reconstruction in 1877, and mainly allied themselves with big business.

A crisis is an opportunity, but it hardly guarantees a successful presidency. For every Franklin Roosevelt, there is a Herbert Hoover. For every Lyndon Johnson turning the civil rights impasse into a moment of national greatness, there is a Jimmy Carter fumbling the energy crisis—or Johnson himself blundering into Vietnam. And on the conservative side, for every Ronald Reagan bringing working-class voters into the Republican coalition and successfully associating national optimism with far-right policies, there is a George W. Bush.

So either Barack Obama will be a transformative president, or the bad economic circumstances that he inherits will sink his promise and America's, and the moment will have been lost. He will be a great president—or a failed one, his presidency grounded "in shallows and in miseries."

The Hope of Audacity

Who, really, is Barack Obama? The moment may cry out for dramatic national change, but why should we think he will be that rare transformational leader? Giving him some benefit of the doubt, there are two basic reasons. First, his personal odyssey, writings, and speeches suggest a capacity to truly move people and shift perceptions as well as bridge differences. Second, they suggest more a principled idealist than a cynic. Anyone who thinks Obama is more weather vane than compass has not carefully read his books, followed his history, or watched him in action. His first book, *Dreams from My Father*, conveyed a depth and self-reflective life journey breathtaking for one still in his early thirties. It suggested Obama's character, and something else absurdly improbable in a thirty-three-year-old—wisdom.

James MacGregor Burns writes, "At the highest stage of moral development, persons are guided by near-universal ethical principles of justice such as human rights and respect for individual dignity. This stage sets the opportunity for rare and creative leadership." Only a handful of American presidents have possessed this gift. Given the desert of inspired political leadership in recent years, people today are thirsty for such a leader.

Obama's supporters believe they discern this potential. Newton Minow, the Chicago liberal warhorse who served in the Kennedy administration, told Obama, "I saw John Kennedy and now I've seen you—and I haven't seen anything quite like it in between." Progressives who backed Obama rather than John Edwards or Hillary Clinton for the Democratic nomination gave Obama a pass on some of the issues. At that stage of the campaign, many positions of Edwards and Clinton were actually a shade more progressive. But the Obama backers saw in him the raw material of transforming leadership, even of greatness.

Obama's second book, *The Audacity of Hope*, written in anticipation of his presidential run, combined a desire to unify and heal with a willingness to take principled risks as a progressive. The book was the opposite of the usual campaign volume written by ghostwriters and carefully scrubbed to send coded messages to the base while blandly reassuring a broader public.

Here is Obama, supposedly packaged as the post-racial African American, the Tiger Woods of American politics, casually sharing a reverie about race, expressing the audacious hope that far more unites Americans than divides them—but doing so with nerve and a refreshing absence of platitudes:

> I imagine the white southerner who growing up heard his dad talk about niggers this and niggers that but who has struck up a friendship with the black guys at the office and is trying to teach his own son different, who thinks discrimination is wrong but doesn't see why the son of a black doctor should be admitted to law school ahead of his own son. Or the former Black Panther who decided to go into real estate, bought a few buildings in the neighborhood, and is just as tired of the drug dealers in front of those buildings as he is of the bankers who won't give him a loan to expand his business.

Deconstruct those two sentences: Yes, there is plenty of ugliness in America's racial history—*niggers this, niggers that*. There are decent whites trying to transcend it, but affirmative action sometimes isn't fair to whites, either. Though the black experience is more brutal, blacks and whites alike have legitimate anxieties about race. Many of the concerns are really about who gets ahead economically. Most blacks don't have any more tolerance for crime than most whites. Redemption is always possible—the white southerner, his black office mates, and his son; the former Black Panther as small businessman. All of this is deeply personal as well as subtle, complicated, and elegant; it's about the struggles of decent people that shouldn't be reduced to slogans and stereotypes.

This is a narrative that speaks to American life as it is lived. It conveys genuine empathy. It is intuitive Obama. No pollster or speechwriter could have composed that passage. The fervent desire to transcend difference is sincere—and hardly surprising in the son of a white Kansan and a black Kenyan. Likewise the wish to reach across the partisan aisle, which reflects Obama's own experience in the Illinois legislature, sometimes moving Republicans to embrace surprisingly progressive policies.

But going forward, will Obama use this political genius as a true progressive? Here the jury is out—though my bet is that economic circumstances will compel nothing less, and that Obama is astute enough to grasp this reality.

During the pre–Labor Day phase of the campaign, however, Obama at times made calculated moves to the center in both his staffing and his positioning—moves that could preclude the kind of transforming policies invoked in his most powerful speeches. In mid-June, Obama named a respected moderate liberal and close protégé of Clinton Treasury secretary Robert Rubin, Jason Furman, as his chief economic adviser. Furman complements an economic centrist on the campaign team, Austan Goolsbee, a friend of Obama's since the days when both taught at the University of Chicago. Goolsbee, during primary season, had brought in two other centrist academic economists, David Cutler of Harvard, who favors "market-based" solutions to the health insurance crisis, and Jeffrey Liebman, an expert on anti-poverty and pension policy, who has supported a partial privatization of Social Security. The most apt words to describe all four are smart and orthodox. However, both Obama himself, and Furman at Obama's direction, reached out to several other economists whose thinking cannot be characterized as orthodox. These included Robert Reich, Jared Bernstein, William Spriggs, and James Galbraith.

After wrapping up the nomination, Obama also hired (and then quickly fired) one of Washington's most blemished insider political operatives, former Fannie Mae CEO Jim Johnson, to head his vice presidential search; he capped the month by hiring Senator Max Baucus's chief aide, Jim Messina, as his own chief of staff. Baucus, more than any other Democrat, was the chief enabler of George W. Bush's upwardly tilted tax cuts, and Baucus has been the prime Democratic impediment to bolder Democratic legislative thinking on health policy, taxes, and trade. On the other hand, Messina's great strengths are loyalty, knowledge of Congress, and tactical acumen. Maybe it's not such a bad idea to cultivate ties to a key legislator in a position to either block or advance a presidential agenda.

Obama then appalled civil libertarians by voting for an administration bill giving immunity to telephone companies that cooperate with warrantless government eavesdropping. He qualified earlier statements on how long the United States would need to keep some troops in Iraq. He reached out to evangelical groups, calling for more "faith-based" delivery of human services, though he did pledge to change the ground rules back to those of the Clinton presidency, which prohibited the use of federal funds to proselytize. He had kind words for an end-of-term Supreme Court decision, written by the high court's conservative bloc, redefining the Second Amendment as creating a right to keep guns in the home. And he even supported a Supreme Court dissent written by Justice Scalia criticizing the majority for not allowing the death penalty for crimes other than murder.

The Wall Street Journal, in a lead editorial, made great sport of Obama's repositioning. "We're beginning to understand why Barack Obama keeps protesting so vigorously against the prospect of 'George Bush's third term.' Maybe he's worried that someone will notice that he's the candidate who's running for it."

Disillusioned *New York Times* columnist Bob Herbert, long smitten by Obama, spoke for many liberals: "Senator Obama is not just tacking gently toward the center. He's lurching right when it suits him, and he's zigging with the kind of reckless abandon that's guaranteed to cause disillusion, if not whiplash."

Can this repositioning be defended? *The New Yorker*'s Hendrik Hertzberg, in a close analysis of these seeming shifts, reported that only the new position on telephone tapping was a genuine reversal. We can appreciate why someone named Barack Hussein Obama, who first won the hearts of liberal activists with an early and brave speech opposing Bush's Iraq War, would want to reassure moderates that he can be trusted with the nation's security. It is also reasonable for a biracial candidate with a Muslim grandfather, one who spent some of his childhood in Indonesia, to go the extra mile in reaching out to white Christians. And one can understand why Obama, as an outsider candidate, would want to build bridges to Democratic insiders right after locking up the nomination.

At times, however, Obama overdid it, and began to undermine his most precious asset—the widespread perception that he is something special, not just another politician. Paradoxically, the perception that he was scuttling to the center hurt him with moderates who admire his independence as well as liberals who admire his convictions.

Obama's efforts to appeal to a broad spectrum as well as his liberal base, however, are not new. In two emblematic passages from *The Audacity of Hope*, Obama writes,

> I am a Democrat, after all; my views on most topics correspond more closely to the editorial pages of the *New York Times* than those of the *Wall Street Journal*. I am angry about policies that consistently favor the wealthy and the powerful over average Americans, and I insist that government has an important role in opening up opportunity to all. I believe in evolution, scientific inquiry, and global warming . . .

But that is not all that I am. I also think my party can be smug, detached, and dogmatic at times. I believe in free markets, competition, and entrepreneurship, and I think no small number of government programs don't work as advertised.

Or again, decrying excessive partisanship,

Depending on your tastes, our condition is the natural result of radical conservatism or perverse liberalism, Tom DeLay or Nancy Pelosi, big oil or greedy trial lawyers, religious zealots or gay activists, Fox News or *The New York Times*. How well these stories are told . . . They are stories of conspiracy, of America being hijacked by an evil cabal . . .

Of course, there is another story to be told, by the millions of Americans who are going about their business every day. They are on the job or looking for work, starting businesses, helping their kids with their homework, and struggling with high gas bills, insufficient health insurance, and a pension that some bankruptcy court somewhere has rendered unenforceable.

What exactly is Obama saying here? He has made an informed judgment that most Americans, even partisans, are sick of partisanship. At the same time, the specific ills that he mentions can fairly be laid at the door of Republicans—the scarcity of good jobs, the unreliable health insurance and vulnerable pensions. Done well, it's a sly subtext, critical of the right, grounded in progressive values, embedded in an appeal to unity.

His critics would say he is trying to have it both ways. On the one hand, he accepts that liberals don't have a monopoly on political wisdom; he is validating the belief that both sides share some responsibility for political blockage. On the other hand, he is pretty clear that the big failures are failures of conservative rule; that he would govern as a progressive, though with tender consideration for some conservative values.

At one point Obama writes, a little disingenuously, "We know that our health-care system is broken . . . But year after year, ideology and political gamesmanship result in inaction, except for 2003, when we got a prescription drug bill that somehow managed to combine the worst aspects of the public and private sectors—price gouging and bureaucratic confusion, gaps in coverage and an eye-popping bill for taxpayers."

Reading that sentence, you get the feeling that Obama assigns roughly symmetrical blame for that outcome. But anyone who followed the issue, Barack Obama included, knows full well that it wasn't "ideology and political gamesmanship" in general that produced such a wretched excuse for a program; it was George W. Bush's cynical, take-it-or-leave-it alliance with the insurance and drug industries that added red tape, inflated costs, and cut net benefits. On the other hand, the bill would not have passed unless conservative Democrats had chosen to be Bush's enablers. So Obama's criticism of both parties had some substance—it was not just calculated positioning as an anti-Washington outsider.

In his analysis of the forces that have blocked reform, Obama has sometimes seemed a little too cagey and too kind to the right—which has been the main source of that blockage. But a progressive with the skill to reassure conservatives and moderates might be just what the national moment requires. After all, as the right keeps shouting from the housetops, Obama really does have the most liberal voting record in the Senate. If he can pull this off—disarming the Republican stereotypes of liberals while not giving away his progressive substance—more power to him.

It is also noteworthy that even in the contest for the Democratic nomination, where the primary and caucus candidates competed for the votes of the most zealous of Democratic partisans, Obama was the one who toned down the partisanship. Even though Obama had the most left-of-center voting record,

John Edwards and Hillary Clinton both offered hotter rhetoric for the Democratic base. But Obama won.

As the campaign progressed, Obama increasingly demonstrated his capacity to be a tough partisan as well as an aspirational unifier. At his best, Obama uses his speeches as occasions to teach, to persuade the country that we need to move in a better direction. His major address on foreign policy and national security, delivered in Washington July 15, was both uplifting and scathing. He began by invoking America's leadership in the post–World War II era—the Marshall Plan and the dawn of the Atlantic Alliance. Then he turned to the attacks on the World Trade Center and Pentagon.

> Imagine, for a moment, what we could have done in those days, and months, and years after 9/11.
>
> We could have deployed the full force of American power to hunt down and destroy Osama bin Laden, al Qaeda, the Taliban, and all of the terrorists responsible for 9/11, while supporting real security in Afghanistan.
>
> We could have secured loose nuclear materials around the world, and updated a 20th century non-proliferation framework to meet the challenges of the 21st.
>
> We could have invested hundreds of billions of dollars in alternative sources of energy to grow our economy, save our planet, and end the tyranny of oil.
>
> We could have strengthened old alliances, formed new partnerships, and renewed international institutions to advance peace and prosperity.
>
> We could have called on a new generation to step into the strong currents of history, and to serve their country as troops and teachers, Peace Corps volunteers and police officers.
>
> We could have secured our homeland—investing in sophisticated new protection for our ports, our trains and our power plants.

We could have rebuilt our roads and bridges, laid down new rail and broadband and electricity systems, and made college affordable for every American to strengthen our ability to compete.

We could have done that.

Instead, we have lost thousands of American lives, spent nearly a trillion dollars, alienated allies and neglected emerging threats—all in the cause of fighting a war for well over five years in a country that had absolutely nothing to do with the 9/11 attacks.

Obama did not mince words in explaining why America under the Republicans had failed to do any of that, and why he could be a very different brand of leader. This speech was not constructed around applause lines or cheap slogans. Like Roosevelt's Fireside Chats or Lincoln's great addresses, the speech suggested a serious mind at work, a leader interested in teaching, a voice with the potential to call America to be its best self. And by late July, as economic conditions worsened, he was proposing bolder economic recovery measures.

Some observers initially viewed Obama as a lucky novice ("Obambi," in Maureen Dowd's oft-repeated put-down)—a sweet naïf who got to where he did based on a smile and a shoeshine. It is increasingly clear that he is no political innocent. As Ryan Lizza wrote in a long *New Yorker* profile, "Obama's rise has often appeared effortless. His offstage tactics—when he is engaged in the sometimes combative work of a politician—are rarely glimpsed by outsiders."

But we should hardly be shocked, much less disillusioned, that Barack Obama turns out to be an effective, shrewd politician. All our great presidents were also superb politicians. One other relatively unknown politician from Illinois startled veteran political observers when he came, seemingly out of nowhere, to wrest a presidential nomination from three better-known and better-situated rivals. "Chance, positioning, and managerial strategy—all played a role in Lincoln's victory," writes Doris Goodwin. "His nomination, finally, was the result of his character and his life experience—these separated him from his rivals and provided him with advantages unrecognized at the time."

It is also worth recalling that prior to the summer of 2008, Barack Obama *had never faced a Republican opponent in a close general election,* making him literally the only major-party presidential nominee in modern times with that hole in his résumé. He brilliantly won an underdog primary in a safe Democratic seat for the Illinois state senate in 1996, and likewise for the US Senate in 2004 (when the GOP nominee had to withdraw because of a sex scandal, leaving the hapless Republicans to import an out-of-state crank, the perennial candidate Alan Keyes, who got just 29 percent of the vote). And his upset victory over Hillary Clinton was won, once again, within in the Democratic Party.

So it is hardly surprising that Obama started out the 2008 campaign believing that you don't have to be a tough *partisan* to be a winning progressive politician—because he has never had to. Yet his partisanship seems to be maturing nicely—without sacrificing his gift for the broad unifying vision.

Lately there have been several books on politics and language, with titles like *The Political Mind, The Political Brain,* and *Talking Right,* as well as thousands of polls, focus groups, and framing and messaging exercises, all intended to help politicians better understand what is vexing voters and how to use words more effectively to move public opinion in this or that direction. Some of these authors offer valuable insights. But I would trade all this expert advice for one elected progressive leader whose political ear has near-perfect pitch.

The Economic Trap

With his talent for leadership, a President Obama could transform American politics on several dimensions. He could restore

America's constructive role in the world. (After Obama's Berlin speech, *New York Times* columnist Frank Rich wondered how long it had been since American children watching TV had seen American flags being waved by foreigners rather than burned.) He could redefine the connection between liberty and security after more than seven years of scare tactics eroding constitutional protections. He could at last lead America to take the climate crisis seriously, and turn us away from a path toward planetary catastrophe. He could finally end the stalemate on the key domestic issue of health reform. He could activate the latent idealism of young people and mobilize an entire generation to be lifelong progressive Democrats, the way Roosevelt did.

He has already transformed attitudes on race and on tolerance, and he has just begun. Despite his own background, Obama paradoxically is a post-racial figure in a society weary of racial division. Both for younger, more tolerant Americans who are electrified by his promise, and for an older generation of more conservative whites skeptical of racial preferences, Obama shines out as the opposite of affirmative action—a biracial African American who, against all odds, succeeded based on sheer merit. After a generation of blacks helped up the ladder by affirmative action, Obama is not a black man who got to his present position thanks to the need for racial symbolism, such as, say, Clarence Thomas. He rather evokes Jackie Robinson—one whose talent was so exceptional that he could not be denied. He is what Americans of goodwill dreamed could occur once we put racism behind us; as Leon Wieseltier memorably put it, not the seed of civil rights but the flower.

But all of this promise could come to naught if Obama fails to address the economic crisis. For Barack Obama and the US economy face the most difficult set of challenges since those that greeted Franklin Roosevelt in March 1933:

- A deepening recession caused by both a traumatized financial system and weakened consumer purchasing power.

- A banking system that will lose between \$1 and \$2 trillion of capital.
- The worst collapse in housing values since the Depression.
- A simultaneous outbreak of worldwide inflation.
- Global constraints—a weak dollar and high foreign debt—on a recovery program reliant mainly on low interest rates (our key policy to date).
- Pre-recession budget deficits already at fairly high levels.
- Widening income insecurity and inequality.
- State and local governments that are short of revenues because tax receipts fall in a recession—at just the moment when demand for public services rises.
- An energy and environmental crisis that demands a dramatically different course.
- A health system that is becoming less reliable and more expensive.

In mid-2007, long-brewing trends turned into economic crisis. In mid-2008, after a year of the government dithering, the financial collapse turned dire.

The backstory is thirty years of steady worsening of the economic condition of ordinary Americans, as government ceased to provide economic balance. The first of these trends has been stagnant or falling living standards, a three-decade pattern that intensified after George W. Bush took office. In the eight years since 2001, only about 5 percent of Americans have enjoyed real income gains adjusted for inflation.

The pattern has been especially severe for the young, who face a much steeper path to secure membership in the middle class than their parents did, given costs of college tuition, decent health insurance, and homeownership. Too many commentators and professional economists attributed these trends to such factors as education or labor-market shifts—to everything but the reversal in government policies that once protected Americans from the vagaries of markets and counterbalanced the influence of great wealth.

During the same period, a revolution occurred in the roles of men and women in the economy. It became normal—and financially necessary—for mothers of small children to join the paid labor force. Between 1979 and 2006, the number of hours worked by the median husband–wife household increased by about 400 per year. Yet during this period, there were no notable changes in the policies either of government or of private corporations to ease the tension between the obligations of work and of family. Government abdicated, and corporations left families to fend for themselves. Raising a family while making ends meet simply became more arduous. And again, a debilitating social pattern that was the consequence of a political failure was seen as beyond politics. Except among the activist class, people experienced these escalating stresses as their own private problems, not defaults of public policy to address changing needs.

And in the years since 1980, risks once borne by large institutions or by government were shifted to individuals and families. A generation ago, stable corporations generally assured their employees reliable careers, decent pensions, adequate health coverage. Government provided social insurance against job loss and poverty in old age. Government also offered the sons and daughters of the working and middle class affordable higher educations through public universities and other forms of college aid. Government subsidized starter homes. As corporations have become more footloose, it would make sense to provide health insurance and pensions socially. Instead, more risks have been shifted to individuals. Here again, those in middle age are more likely to enjoy the remnants of these traditional protections while the young are more likely to go without.

Depressed Economy, Depressed Expectations

These economic reversals, however, did not produce a political counter-revolution—until now. One reason: They occurred slowly, unlike the abrupt onset of the Great Depression. The result was a "frog-in-the-saucepan" effect. (It is said, based on laboratory experiments first performed in the 1870s, that if you put a frog in a pot of hot water, he will jump out; but if you turn up the heat very gradually, he will poach to death.) People blamed their slowly worsening circumstances on themselves rather than coming together in a movement for political change.

Another reason: Democrats stopped being the party of credible activist government. Central to the voter passivity was lowered expectations. In all of these transitions that increased the economic insecurity of ordinary Americans, government provided little if any help.

For twenty of the past twenty-eight years, the occupant of the White House was a conservative Republican, and the idea that government should keep hands off the economy conformed to Republican ideology. For eight of those years, the incumbent was a centrist Democrat. Except for a brief and failed effort to secure universal health insurance in 1993, the Clinton administration's main preoccupations were fiscal. Small wonder that by 2008 the proposition that government could serve as a counterweight to the insecurities of a market economy had lost credibility. Indeed, I have heard accounts from several leaders of focus groups that downwardly mobile voters, when asked whether they believed that government might improve their lot, break into laughter.

Absent government remediation, citizens have become increasingly skeptical about government's capacity to achieve much of anything—a conclusion carefully nurtured by conservative policies and ideology, and incidentally reinforced by conservative incompetence and corruption in the management of the government. When George W. Bush contends that you can't trust government, his own administration provides the exclamation point. And too many Democrats have reinforced these assumptions rather than contest them.

With economic ills largely depoliticized, Democrats did not play to their strong suit. Leading Democrats could not quite decide whether to champion popular frustrations with bold remedies, or to become Republican-lite. Presidential candidates Kerry, Gore, Dukakis, and Mondale failed to inspire. Clinton, the exception, won election in a three-way race with just 43 percent of the vote and then repeated much of the Republican story about government being the problem. But Obama, at his best, portends something different.

Obama's challenge is to reverse the thirty-year trend not just of Republican rule but of voter quiescence and Democratic complicity. He must raise expectations—and then rise to meet them. More than anything else, he needs to rehabilitate the constructive role of government, both in the minds of the people and in what government delivers. For in the current economic crisis, there is no alternative to the redemption of government to serve a broad common good.

Financial Collapse as a Teachable Moment

On top of three decades of increasing economic insecurity, we now have the most severe financial crisis since the Great Depression and a deepening general recession. As I have explained in my book *The Squandering of America* (2007), this crisis is the needless result of too much deregulation—too much private-sector mischief, too little government counterweight. Behind the deregulation was the pervasive ideology of laissez-faire and the political power of the business class. The effects are still cascading. And while restoration of normal financial regulation is overdue, that reform by itself will not reverse the accumulated damage.

A much weakened financial system has produced a credit contraction that low interest rates can only ameliorate, not cure.

By now, banks have lost something like $1 trillion. And since the banking system is based on lending money at multiples of bank capital, without the government's bailing bucket the potential effect on the real economy is closer to $10 trillion. As shareholders avoid investing in banks, the value of banking stocks declines, reducing the capital footings against which banks can lend. The downward spiral continues. Only Roosevelt-scale intervention can reverse this slide.

Three decades of economic negligence by political and financial elites have also weakened the United States globally. Where we once were net providers of capital to the rest of the world, we are now a net debtor. Every year, America imports about 6 percent of GDP more than we export. We borrow most of the rest. Half of America's public debt of $5.6 trillion is now held by foreigners—almost half of that by the central banks of China and Japan. And our private capital markets are increasingly reliant on foreign owners, the fastest-growing component being "sovereign wealth funds," many of which are held by nations that share neither our professed views of free markets nor the basic tenets of our liberal democracy. With the exception of Norway, whose national oil fund is a model of democratic transparency, many of these sovereign wealth funds are the state-owned booty of dictatorships.

The rate of negative change is unprecedented. Just twenty years ago in 1988, the foreign share of America's total national debt was just 13 percent. As recently as 1985, the United States had a net positive investment balance with the rest of the world. But our net national investment position has gone from a negative $360 billion in 1997 to a negative $3.4 trillion—a tenfold worsening in a decade. With a trade deficit of about $700 billion a year and national savings rates close to zero, we add roughly that sum to our negative international balance every year.

These international imbalances created the preconditions for a weakening dollar—and the dollar slide turned into a rout once the subprime collapse turned critical. Foreign central banks have announced policies of diversifying their currency holdings, which will only further weaken the value of the dollar.

Consumer spending is ordinarily the engine of economic growth. As incomes have stagnated, consumer purchasing power was sustained by debt bubbles. In the late 1990s, the inflated stock market led people to feel richer. They borrowed rather than saved. These "wealth effects," according to the Federal Reserve, increased consumer spending by hundreds of billions a year and reduced consumer savings rates to almost nothing. After the stock market collapsed in the early years of this decade, inflated housing prices played the same role. According to a technical study co-authored by no less than Alan Greenspan, home equity withdrawals accounted for 3 percent of consumer purchasing power between 2001 and 2005. And if you include profits extracted from the sale of homes, the figure equaled more than 10 percent of annual consumer buying power.

Now, with unemployment increasing, the stock market in bear territory, housing prices in decline, and wages falling behind inflation, consumers cannot use their homes as a general piggy bank, because the subprime collapse has triggered both a decline in housing values and a tightening of credit standards. So consumers have taken a quadruple hit—falling real wages, declining home equity values, a deteriorating stock market, and skyrocketing energy costs. And increasing inflation is always bad for stocks and bonds.

As the new administration dawns, a repeat of the "stagflation" experience of the 1970s looms: the anomalous coexistence of rising inflation with worsening recession. As of July 2008, the annual inflation rate was running at 5.6 percent. Then as now, at the center of the story is oil. As the subprime crisis prompted the Federal Reserve to drastically cut interest rates, the fall in the value of the US dollar accelerated. Since oil is priced internationally in dollars, the oil-producing nations reacted by raising prices. Those hikes function as a heavy tax on the rest of the economy and exacerbate the trade imbalance.

A weak dollar coincided with rising demand for oil and food from emergent economies such as China and India, compounded by the purchases of speculators looking for substitutes for the deflated bubbles in stocks and housing. After the economy returned to price stability in the late 1980s and 1990s following the oil shocks of the 1970s, the inflation-adjusted price of oil subsided. But that is much less likely to happen today, because worldwide oil production is near or past its peak. And of course, the environmental pressures of global climate change suggest that even if more oil could be discovered, we need to drastically reduce our dependence on it and other carbon-based fuels, through either higher real prices or other deliberate strategies.

Breaking the Frame

As this book will explain, all of these problems have solutions. But before Barack Obama can address them as president, he must first break free of the undertow of bad ideas. Even though his own party will have the largest working majority in Congress enjoyed by a Democratic president in three decades (with the possible exception of Clinton's first two years), the Democrats are divided when it comes to the expansive use of affirmative government to restore decent living standards and promote a general economic recovery. And of course the Republicans are dead opposed. Only strong presidential leadership can overcome these divisions.

While Democrats have long been intimidated by the "tax-and-spend" label, most have now accepted the need to restore taxes on the top brackets. Obama and his chief rival, Hillary Clinton, both campaigned on a platform to raise taxes on people with annual earnings of at least $250,000, roughly the wealthiest 2 percent of Americans. Both pledged to reclaim at least some inheritance taxes on very large estates.

However, when it comes to deciding what to do with this revenue, Democrats are badly split. Some would like to see the larger role for government and restoration of robust public investment that this book commends, especially in a deep recession. But others, such as the forty-nine-member House "Blue Dog" caucus, are fiscal conservatives. Most are willing to raise taxes but want to strictly balance the federal budget, and many hope to cut spending. Cousin to the Blue Dogs is the party faction that takes its lead from Robert Rubin, the former Clinton Treasury secretary. Rubin places top priority on capping the costs of so-called entitlement programs such as Social Security and Medicare and sharply reducing the current deficit, tempered by only modest spending increases. This group, illustrated by the work of Rubin's Hamilton Project, favors fiscal restraint, some tax increases on the wealthy, and very modest spending increases.

The Hamilton Project, whose director until June 2008 was Jason Furman, is an ad hoc think tank based at the Brookings Institution. If you visit the project's Web site, you will find bold rhetoric on the need for both fiscal discipline and public outlay, coupled with the most modest of spending proposals. The general premise of the Hamilton group is that social outlays should be reconfigured, but that net spending increases should be minimal. The British have a nice expression for this kind of bargain—horse and rabbit stew, a seemingly equal ragout made of one horse and one rabbit. In the Hamilton Project's policy stew, fiscal discipline is the horse and social outlay the rabbit.

Obama's own economic proposals to date have sometimes mocked his bold rhetoric. On July 7, with a good deal of fanfare, Obama delivered a speech titled "An Agenda for Middle Class Success." He began well by describing the Republican philosophy: "Give massive tax breaks to big corporations and multimillionaires and hope that prosperity trickles down to everyone else. Sacrifice investments in health care and education and energy and technology to pay for these tax breaks, and borrow the rest from countries like China, leaving our children to foot the bill." And he added, "Well it's painfully clear by now how badly this strategy has failed. And this is a fundamental issue in this campaign, because Senator McCain and I have very different views of where our economy is today, and where we need to go."

But the program he laid out, little that wasn't already on his campaign Web site, was pretty weak tea: a middle-class tax cut of $1,000 per worker; additional tax cuts for retired people; a second stimulus package of $50 billion; a new mortgage tax credit; a credit card holders' Bill of Rights; a rather piecemeal approach to health reform; portable 401(k) retirement plans; and kindred rather small-bore proposals. In deference to fiscal conservatives, Obama also pledged that "all my new spending proposals would be more than paid for by spending reductions."

The problem with this formula is that *it will not fix what is broken*. Greater fiscal discipline coupled with modest tax breaks and token spending increases will not produce a recovery from the current recession, much less a restoration of the economic security and depleted earning power of the American middle class. On July 31, with a worsening economy and unemployment up again, Obama proposed a much bolder $50 billion emergency recovery program that moves in the right direction, though not far enough. Chapter 4 of this book provides an alternative economic strategy that would accomplish recovery and restored security, primarily using the power of public investment. But for now, just consider some sober economic facts.

Unemployment at this writing is 5.7 percent, and rising. Between January and June, the economy lost 438,000 net jobs, and layoffs accelerated in July. Counting people who have been involuntarily cut to part-time work, the rate is close to 10 percent. The rising price of oil caused massive losses for airlines and automakers. American homeowners have lost more than $2 trillion in the value of their homes, home equity borrowings have sharply contracted, and foreclosures are now running at 25,000 a month. State governments have lost over $40 billion in antici-pated revenues in 2008 alone. Their 2008 budgets were devised in 2007, on the assumption of $2-per-gallon gasoline. Energy costs have increased by several hundred billion dollars over 2007.

Banks are reeling not from old-fashioned runs by depositors but panic selling by shareholders, which further depletes their capital. The "stimulus package" enacted early in 2008, totaling $168 billion, gave taxpayers average rebates of a few hundred dollars. This did not even cover the out-of-pocket increases in the cost of energy—so there was no net stimulus at all.

In these circumstances, only one general policy approach can dig the economy out of its current hole and put it back on a path toward broadly shared prosperity: Restore taxes on corporations and the wealthiest Americans, reduce spending on foreign wars, incur temporary larger deficits, and use the proceeds for very substantial social investments. This means not just a "stimulus" as a onetime, counter-cyclical injection of demand, but a structural increase in government outlay to make the economy both more productive and more reliable for citizens.

In general, most Democrats and the Obama campaign as of August 2008 have assumed that they could come up with something like $100 to $150 billion per year in additional public outlay through tax increases on the well-to-do and some kind of peace dividend as we limit America's military presence in Iraq. The problem is that this sum—less than 1 percent of GDP—is far too small to make a difference.

As this book will argue, an economic recovery will require more like $700 billion a year in new public outlay, or $600 billion counting offsetting cuts in military spending. Why? Because there is no other plausible strategy for both achieving a general economic recovery and restoring balance to the economy. This is an order-of-magnitude number; we may need even more; we could make do with a little less. What could $700 billion a year buy?

Among other things, the money could be invested in energy independence by subsidizing demand for renewable energy, accelerating technological breakthroughs, and underwriting an extensive program for retrofitting buildings and other strategies of energy efficiency. Building a post-petroleum economy would also improve our trade balance and create new industries and good jobs.

Some of the money could go for outlays on long-deferred basic public infrastructure. The American Society of Civil Engineers calculates that we have $1.6 trillion in deferred basic public investment—in such things as bridges, roads, and schools. With rising energy costs, in addition to repairing crumbling infrastructure, we need a new generation of rail and other mass transit. Public works investment can increase the nation's productivity and produce millions of good jobs. It demonstrates visible public improvements and the beneficial role of government.

A third use of the new public outlay would be to restore America's social contract and bring it into the twenty-first century. This would include finally creating a national system of high-quality child care and universal pre-kindergarten, as well as universal health insurance. Another good candidate for public outlay is the restoration of affordable higher education and first-time homeownership, as well as a refinancing and mortgage-subsidy strategy to brake the slide in housing prices.

We also need a national commitment to the proposition that every job in the human services should be a good job. About 60 percent of all spending on the care of the young, the old, and the sick is ultimately public spending, through either direct income transfers or indirect subsidies. This is a sector whose jobs cannot be moved offshore. But far too many of these jobs are very low-wage, low-skill, high-turnover jobs. If we had a national policy that every single job caring for our aged parents and our young children was defined as a professional, living-wage job, we could create many millions of good jobs in the service sector. At the same time, we could ease the lives of the elderly and give all of America's children a healthy start, and their mothers and fathers more capacity to be both productive workers and nurturing parents.

Commitments on this scale, unlike so many of the purely token government initiatives of recent decades, would deliver tangible help to economically stressed middle- and working-class Americans. They would restore the practical bond between citizen and government and break through the prevailing cynicism.

They would signal the boldness of national endeavor. Many of these aspirations are in Obama's speeches. But they are undercut by the fine print of fiscal orthodoxy.

Where on earth could the federal government get an additional $600 billion a year? This task is not as daunting as it first seems. It would not require increasing taxes on anyone earning less than $250,000. So roughly the bottom 98 percent of the population would be unaffected.

The details of this program are spelled out in chapter 4, but here are the major ways to pay for it:

Restoring the tax code to its structure before the Bush tax cuts, while retaining the tax breaks that benefited the non-rich, would produce about $150 billion a year, net. In addition, the consensus among tax experts is that at least $300 billion of taxes owed by the richest Americans go uncollected mainly because IRS enforcement resources have been diverted from audits of tax shelters used only by the wealthy onto audits of working Americans. Next, a modest estimate of the money that could be redirected from winding down America's entanglements in Iraq totals $100 billion a year (and more in years to come). And a very small transactions tax on purely speculative activity would yield another $100 billion a year. This would not only raise needed revenue but also moderate the kind of dangerous financial engineering that led to the subprime collapse. All this adds up to $650 billion a year, and virtually nobody earning less than $250,000 under this scheme pays more tax. The entire fiscal shift need not come in the first year.

What about deficit spending? As this book was going to press, the Office of Management and Budget sharply revised its deficit projections upward, to $482 billion in fiscal year 2009. That's about 3.3 percent of GDP. Deficits normally increase in recessions because economic activity shrinks and revenues fall. This deficit is compounded by bad tax and military policy, and the beginnings of large-scale government rescues such as the Fannie Mae–Freddie Mac bailout. But deficit spending is needed in a recession, and these are not per se scary numbers despite a lot of scare-mongering. The total national debt held by the public is a very manageable 37 percent of GDP—a lower percentage than for the entire post–World War II boom. If that ratio needs to increase to, say, 45 or 50 percent to cure this economic crisis, it can again resume its downward trend once the economy is in recovery, just as occurred in the postwar boom.

Over the business cycle, the federal budget does not need to be balanced. As long as we can restore economic growth to something like a normal level of about 3 percent a year, a public deficit averaging around 2 percent of GDP can be sustained indefinitely. The deficit itself is far less of a concern than the reliance on capricious foreign investors to finance it.

Fiscal conservatives have faulted the Bush administration for adding to federal deficits. However, the problem with Bush's budget is not the size of the deficit, but its makeup. Bush's deficit is built on gratuitous tax cuts for the very rich and a needless war. If the same deficit were the consequence of a fairer tax code and increased social investment that made the economy more productive and more fair, the current net deficit would be entirely virtuous. The Bush tax cuts were supposed to lead to increased private investment, higher savings rates, and improved economic growth. Their effect was precisely the opposite.

The value of raising taxes on the wealthy and investing the money socially is that every penny goes for short- and long-term economic stimulus for general benefit instead of wealth hoarding, speculation abroad, and luxury consumption for a tiny few. As I am working on this chapter, three articles from the front page of *The New York Times* bring this news: Leona Helmsley's lightly taxed estate left as much as $8 billion in trust accounts for dogs. Richard Grasso, former CEO of the New York Stock Exchange, at the time a nonprofit institution with many public regulatory functions, won his court battle to keep $139.5 million in windfall pay awarded by his cronies on the stock exchange board. And the lead story: "Deepening Cycle of Job Loss Seen Lasting into '09."

It doesn't take a Roosevelt to connect these dots. But it does take more leadership and political nerve than we've seen lately.

The Character of Transformation

A program of increased social outlay along the lines that I describe is necessary to put the economy on the road to balanced recovery. But it is not the whole of a recovery program. The other large economic policy areas crying out for dramatic change are in the realms of regulation, trade, labor, and global energy and environment policy. I will have more to say on this in chapters 4 and 5.

President Obama will need to break with the bipartisan conventions of extreme financial deregulation, which led to the subprime crisis, the credit crunch, the slide in housing values, and the weakening of bank balance sheets—which in turn supercharged general recession. Deregulated financial markets also create a needless Hobson's choice for central bankers: Either let banks suffer the folly of their own mistakes and risk having a financial crisis turn into a general depression; or keep bailing out banks and invite more speculative bubbles. But obviously, there is a third alternative: Complement necessary rescues with much more stringent supervision and regulation, so that speculative bubbles stop occurring. As Obama himself put it in a brilliant speech at Cooper Union last March 27,

> Our history should give us confidence that we don't have to choose between an oppressive government-run economy and a chaotic and unforgiving capitalism. It tells us we can emerge from great economic upheavals stronger, not weaker.
>
> We need to regulate institutions for what they do, not what they are. Over the last few years, commercial banks and thrift institutions were subject to guidelines on subprime mortgages that did not apply to mortgage

brokers and companies. It makes no sense for the Fed to
tighten mortgage guidelines for banks when two-thirds
of subprime mortgages don't originate from banks. This
regulatory framework has failed to protect homeowners,
and it is now clear that it made no sense for our financial
system.

Obama went on to call for tough regulations against financial
conflicts of interest, going far beyond the conventional wisdom
of his own party. This is the stuff of transformation—because it
educates the people and puts the leader on the side of profound
change. This kind of nervy speech should reassure those who fear
that Obama is becoming a captive of his staff. He is well known for
reaching out to a very broad range of thinkers. Roosevelt, before
him, would exasperate his closest advisers by having conversations with people nobody had ever heard of. Obama is also astute
at learning from mistakes and making course corrections.

His Cooper Union speech did not reflect the views of centrist
advisers. Well-placed sources have told me that it was informed
by Obama's conversations with a range of less orthodox economic
thinkers, including former Treasury official Daniel Tarullo, former
Fed Chairman Paul Volcker, and Warren Buffett. (Volcker overdid the anti-inflation shock therapy in the 1970s, but he is a
fierce and well-informed critic of financial excesses.)

Obama has cited Doris Kearns Goodwin's book on Lincoln,
Team of Rivals, as an influence on how he intends to govern—to
appoint an ideologically diverse set of advisers and listen carefully to all the arguments before coming to his own conclusions.
The best presidents have done just that. President Kennedy over-
ruled several of his military advisers in heading off World War III
in his handling of the Cuban Missile Crisis. Franklin Roosevelt
delighted in playing aides against one another to the consterna-
tion of all but himself. Obama reads widely and is well known for
putting advisers with diverse views in a room, and leading a lively
discussion of alternatives.

Quite independent of their appointees, great presidents tend to become more expansive in office, especially when conditions demand it. Lincoln at first did not want to issue an Emancipation Proclamation, because his top priority was preserving the Union. The Civil War became a moral crusade against slavery only over time, and after Lincoln felt he had built a consensus in the North. Lyndon Johnson took his time moving on the Voting Rights Act as he built support in the country and the Congress. Literally from his first week in office, Johnson vowed to be remembered as the president who delivered the century-delayed promise of full civil rights. But it took the murders of Freedom Summer 1964, the August Democratic Convention battles in Atlantic City over whether to seat the integrated delegation of the Mississippi Freedom Democratic Party, and escalating voting rights demonstrations and more official brutality the following winter before Johnson finally decided in early 1965 to put the full moral and constitutional authority of his office and his political mastery behind a national law to give the federal government the power to guarantee voting rights in the South, a feat that had been deemed politically impossible. And of course, Franklin Roosevelt famously campaigned on a platform to balance the budget—before he took office and grasped that circumstances required serious deficit spending.

If a President Obama does embrace a more radical economic recovery program, the reason will be that *economic conditions leave him few other good choices.* And unless he is a far weaker man than his entire life suggests, his original team of cautious advisers will not be able to stand in his way. Those early campaign gestures to the center will be a minor footnote.

If he is to change America, Obama will also need to pay great attention to sequencing, priorities, and the logic of large transformations that begin as incremental reforms. As a onetime community organizer trained in the tradition of Saul Alinsky, Obama knows well that you begin with achievable successes. That creates confidence in the possibility of changes, and paves the way for bigger successes.

Notwithstanding the extraordinary achievements of Franklin Roosevelt's First Hundred Days and Lyndon Johnson's stunning Great Society Congress after his landslide victory in 1964, the more typical experience of incoming Democratic presidents has been that of John Kennedy, Jimmy Carter, and Bill Clinton. Kennedy was largely stymied by southern conservatives in his own party. Jimmy Carter had sixty-one Democratic senators and the second largest Democratic House majority since Roosevelt, but he failed to use it. Clinton decided to put deficit reduction first, alienated much of his own party by making NAFTA a priority, and fumbled the potentially transformative popular issue that helped get him elected, health insurance "that can never be taken away."

However, as we will see in the succeeding chapters, never underestimate the capacity of a great president to mobilize public opinion. Abraham Lincoln wisely said, "With public sentiment, nothing can fail; without it, nothing can succeed. Consequently he who moulds public sentiment goes deeper than he who enacts statutes or pronounces decisions."

It has been a long time—more than four decades—since we have seen a president animate the people on behalf of expansive uses of progressive government. Before turning in detail to the needed economic recovery program, it is worth looking back to explore how transformative presidents used their high office to inspire and achieve durable change, and to appreciate how all great presidents are works in progress.

| two |

How Transformative Presidents Lead

> I mean by leadership not only the transactional leaders who thrive on bargaining, accommodating, and manipulating within a given system, but the transforming leaders who respond to fundamental human needs and wants, hopes and expectations, and who may transcend and even seek to reconstruct the political system rather than simply to operate within it.
>
> —JAMES MACGREGOR BURNS

> Our critical situation is chiefly due to men who try to please the citizens rather than telling them what they need to hear.
>
> —DEMOSTHENES, rallying resistance among the Athenians against Philip of Macedon, 351 BC

What can Obama learn from great transformational presidents? What mistakes should he avoid, learning from presidents whom history offered a transformative moment, but who did not catch the wave? And can a Barack Obama lead like a Franklin Roosevelt absent a Roosevelt-scale crisis? To bring some historical perspective to these questions, consider the bleak winter of 1933, a time when one American in four was unemployed, the financial system was collapsing, and the general mood was less of popular revolt than quiet despair.

Compared with Obama, Roosevelt began with one big advantage and one big disadvantage. The advantage, if we can call it that, was that nobody doubted America was in crisis. The huge disadvantage: This was uncharted economic territory and nobody knew what to do. Roosevelt's historic task was not just to figure out how to proceed, but to define the crisis in a way that built optimism that help was on the way, and then to begin delivering that help. Though conditions today are not as dire as in 1933, Obama's challenge will be to give public definition to what Americans have been experiencing as largely private struggles, and restore a sense of collective possibility.

For Americans who did not live through the Depression, the New Deal has faded into an chronicle of epic inevitability almost as if it were all predestined—the First Hundred Days, the bank holiday, deposit insurance, public works spending, Social Security—a parade of achievements and a restoration of confidence made possible by a desperate economic situation, a large Democratic majority in Congress, and an inspirational new leader.

The reality, of course, was far messier and less assured. There was no single blueprint—the New Deal was cobbled together on the fly. Apart from professional historians and careful students of the Roosevelt era, few Americans today appreciate the factional disputes, the missteps, and the surprising degree to which Roosevelt began by embracing ideas opposite from what we now know as the New Deal. Pressed by events, by progressives in Congress and social movements for change, he was the rare president who became more radical in office.

As Doris Goodwin observes, in 1860 Lincoln was not yet the historical Lincoln we know, and in early 1933 Roosevelt was far from Roosevelt. Even during his successful four-year tenure as governor of New York, most of Roosevelt's contemporaries in the late 1920s considered FDR an affable lightweight. He had a reputation as a trimmer. He was on both sides of the tariff issue, on whether to reform Tammany Hall, whether to repeal Prohibition, whether to go off the gold standard. A fellow Harvard alumnus taunted him as the 4-P's Candidate: Pusillanimously-Pussyfooting-Pious-Platitudinous Roosevelt. Herbert Hoover, in a rare fit of eloquence, called Roosevelt "a chameleon on Scotch plaid."

Later, as he firmed his ideological footings, this penchant for trying out a sampler of sometimes contradictory ideas, often from rival advisers, served Roosevelt well. He was the great experimenter. "Governments can err, Presidents do make mistakes," he famously said, "but the immortal Dante tells us that divine justice weighs the sins of the cold-blooded and the sins of the warm-hearted in different scales. Better the occasional faults of a Government that lives in a spirit of charity than the constant omission of a Government frozen in the ice of its own indifference." And as he gained confidence and experience as president, FDR developed a surer sense of which ideas were sound.

There is no small echo of these traits, positive and negative, in Barack Obama. He talks to a broad range of advisers. He has the self-confidence and the intellect to hear diverse views and then to make up his own mind. He tacks left, as in his call to increase taxes on the affluent and re-regulate Wall Street, and also right, as in piecemeal approach to health reform. In his legislative record to date, however, Obama has ended up on the progressive side far more often than not.

Like the Roosevelt of 1932 and early 1933, many of the ideas proposed by Obama in the pre–Labor Day phase of the 2008 campaign either were too weak to fix economic and financial failures, or fell well short of the historic need to rally the American people to a new era of common purpose. Those seeking historical reassurance should consider some of the ideas on which Roosevelt campaigned—and even governed early months in his first term.

The Forgotten Roosevelt

Most of us dimly recall the irony that FDR the candidate supported a balanced budget. But Roosevelt's orthodox views went much further. In September 1932, campaigning in Sioux City, Iowa, Roosevelt declared, "I accuse the present administration of being the greatest spending Administration in peace times in all our history." In October in Pittsburgh, he pledged, "I regard reduction in federal spending as one of the most important issues of this campaign." The renowned New Deal historian William Leuchtenburg quotes the populist banker Marriner Eccles, whom FDR later appointed to chair the Federal Reserve, "Given later developments, the campaign speeches often read like a giant misprint, in which Roosevelt and Hoover speak each other's lines."

As a candidate, Roosevelt proposed a 25-percent cut in federal outlay—in the depth of the Depression. In his first week as president he actually enacted a short-lived spending cut of *31 percent,* mostly at the expense of veterans and war widows. Almost at the moment Eleanor Roosevelt was graciously serving coffee to the encampment of starving bonus marchers demanding increased pension aid, Franklin was reducing their benefits. "Under the leadership of Franklin Roosevelt," wrote Leuchtenburg, "the budget balancers won a victory for orthodox finance that had not been possible under Hoover." Large-scale social outlay would come only later.

The New Deal is remembered for its profusion of public works. Yet at the outset, Roosevelt was a skeptic. He doubted there were sufficient worthwhile projects, and he abhorred government waste. He did have one pet project, however: conservation and reclamation efforts to put idle city youth to work in the country in military-style camps—cutting brush, building trails, draining swamps, reclaiming rivers, fighting forest fires, improving national parks, and above all planting trees. He believed deeply in conservation and in the virtues of fresh air. This became the famed Civilian Conservation Corps, whose 3 million members eventually planted 3 billion trees.

The CCC, beginning with 250,000 job slots and pay of just a dollar a day, was initially Roosevelt's only proposed program of work relief. The unions feared that it would further depress wages. But Labor Secretary Frances Perkins, a Roosevelt favorite, was relentless in her campaign for much larger-scale public works with better pay, as were several progressive senators and congressmen.

Roosevelt soon became a convert. By the end of his third week in office, he was backpedaling from his budget-balance pledge, distinguishing between a "normal" budget and an "emergency" fiscal situation. (His budget director would later resign in protest over the deficit spending.) Roosevelt's relief legislation, sent to Congress on March 21, included not just the CCC but also the much larger Public Works Administration; the Civil Works Administration, which placed workers directly on the federal payroll with decent wages; and the Federal Emergency Relief Administration.

Within ten months, CWA alone was employing more than 4.2 million people, pumping a billion dollars into the economy, and building roads, schools, and public buildings that exist to this day. By January 1935, the even larger WPA was authorized to spend $5 billion—all this from a champion of budget balance. As Roosevelt reflected on how to handle his flagrant reversal on deficit spending, his adviser Sam Rosenman deadpanned, "Just deny you were ever in Pittsburgh."

Roosevelt also saved the banking system, first with an emergency closure of all the nation's banks (which FDR prettified with the label "bank holiday"), followed by a quick sorting out of which ones were strong enough to reopen, and then with his most important confidence-restoring departure—federal deposit insurance. The idea of the government insuring private bank savings was opposed by fiscal conservatives. But few Americans recall that its fiercest opponents included Roosevelt himself.

In Congress, deposit insurance was promoted by moderate Republicans led by Senator Arthur Vandenburg of Michigan and populist Democrats concerned about small-town banks led by Representative Henry Steagall of Alabama. As the omnibus banking reform legislation, later known as the Glass-Steagall Act, was making its way through the Senate, both Roosevelt and Senator Carter Glass were furious to be outmaneuvered by

Vandenburg, who tacked on a deposit-insurance provision that proved too popular to dislodge. To add insult to injury, Vice President Garner, presiding over the Senate, helped Vandenburg outflank Roosevelt. After threatening to veto the entire bill, Roosevelt reluctantly went on to sign Glass-Steagall. Thanks to deposit insurance, fewer banks failed during the entire remainder of the Depression than in the best year of the Roaring Twenties.

In the banking crisis, Roosevelt did something else that established the tenor of his entire presidency. He asked for the people's help. He didn't ask for "sacrifice"—the people had already sacrificed plenty. Indeed, it is too far easy for comfortable commentators to urge presidents to exhort struggling citizens to further sacrifice. What Roosevelt sought—and got—was the people's collaboration. And he ennobled that endeavor by continuously appealing to the generosity of the citizenry and America's higher purpose.

In his first radio address, Sunday evening, March 12, 1933, a format that would forever after be known as a Fireside Chat, Roosevelt explained the banking crisis in terms that ordinary people could understand—what had happened, how the government was acting to remedy the problem, and how he needed ordinary Americans to do their part. An estimated 60 million people, more than one adult in two, heard the fourteen-minute talk, which is a model of how a president can lead by teaching.

"My friends," he began, "I want to talk for a few minutes with the people of the United States about banking." He added, "I owe this in particular because of the fortitude and good temper with which everybody has accepted the inconvenience and hardships of the banking holiday. I know that when you understand what we in Washington have been about, I shall continue to have your cooperation as fully as I have had your sympathy and help during the past week."

And Roosevelt went on to explain how the banking system works, and the government's plan to reopen most banks as soon as their soundness could be verified.

First of all let me state the simple fact that when you deposit money in a bank the bank does not put the money into a safe deposit vault. It invests your money in many different forms of credit-bonds, commercial paper, mortgages and many other kinds of loans. In other words, the bank puts your money to work to keep the wheels of industry and of agriculture turning around. A comparatively small part of the money you put into the bank is kept in currency—an amount which in normal times is wholly sufficient to cover the cash needs of the average citizen . . .

What, then, happened during the last few days of February and the first few days of March? Because of undermined confidence on the part of the public, there was a general rush by a large portion of our population to turn bank deposits into currency or gold—a rush so great that the soundest banks could not get enough currency to meet the demand. The reason for this was that on the spur of the moment it was, of course, impossible to sell perfectly sound assets of a bank and convert them into cash except at panic prices far below their real value.

"Your Government," Roosevelt pledged, "does not intend that the history of the past few years shall be repeated. We do not want and will not have another epidemic of bank failures." And then he asked for the people's help.

Let me make it clear that the banks will take care of all needs—and it is my belief that hoarding during the past week has become an exceedingly unfashionable pastime. It needs no prophet to tell you that when the people find that they can get their money—that they can get it when they want it for all legitimate purposes—the phantom of fear will soon be laid . . . I can assure you that it is safer to keep your money in a reopened bank than under the mattress.

The success of our whole great national program depends, of course, upon the cooperation of the public—on its intelligent support and use of a reliable system.

We had a bad banking situation. Some of our bankers had shown themselves either incompetent or dishonest in their handling of the people's funds . . . It was the Government's job to straighten out this situation and do it as quickly as possible—and the job is being performed.

FDR concluded:

You people must have faith; you must not be stampeded by rumors or guesses. Let us unite in banishing fear. We have provided the machinery to restore our financial system; it is up to you to support and make it work . . . Together we cannot fail.

He spoke with compassion and good humor, with optimism tempered by realism, and without a trace of condescension. He was even wry; hoarding money was not morally wrong, just "unfashionable." The next morning, a Monday, the people—who had not exactly borne the bank closures with the good humor that Roosevelt ascribed to them—took their money out of mattresses, savings that they could ill afford to lose. And for the first time since the banking panic had begun, they lined up at teller windows not to demand withdrawals but to make deposits—$300 million in a single day.

In that first Fireside Chat, Roosevelt did several things. He made clear that that the private market had failed, and that government help was on the way. He established himself as leader of the government, and in that role as the champion of ordinary Americans who were suffering through no fault of their own. It would be seven long years before the country finally pulled out of the Depression, but the people had a friend in the White

House, one who took the opportunity to remind the citizens that laissez-faire had failed them and that government was the source of help.

From the moment of his inaugural, letters and telegrams poured into the White House, at the rate of about 8,000 a day. Hoover had one assistant to handle his mail from the citizenry. Roosevelt had to hire fifty. His sense of constructive movement was contagious. Before Roosevelt, depression was not just an economic condition; it was a national state of mind. Two weeks after FDR took office, historian Leuchtenburg reports that on the wall of the firm Thomas A. Edison, Inc., in West Orange, New Jersey, the company president, Charles Edison, put up a notice of his own composition that perfectly captured the nation's changed spirit:

> President Roosevelt has done his part: now you do something.
>
> Buy something—buy anything, anywhere; paint your kitchen, send a telegram, give a party, get a car, pay a bill, rent a flat, fix your roof, get a haircut, see a show, build a house, take a trip, sing a song, get married.
>
> It does not matter what you do—but get going and keep going. This old world is starting to move.

As he settled in to his new job, Roosevelt gradually became the man we now think of as *Roosevelt*. Prodded by his own far-flung advisers and by more radical groupings in the Congress and the country (many of which entirely disagreed with one another)—and sometimes restrained by forces of financial orthodoxy—Roosevelt managed to keep his jaunty spirit, gain infectious confidence, and plot his own course. He was able to surf the crosscurrents with a surer and surer touch. There would still be missteps. As late as 1937, he would overrule his advisers and hatch a disastrous scheme to pack the Supreme Court. But the people's trust and affection for FDR were never in doubt, and his leadership on behalf of the proposition that government exists to help ordinary Americans survived Roosevelt by more than a quarter century.

Kennedy and Johnson: From Impasse to Transformation

Obama at his best has a gift common to Lincoln, Roosevelt, and the Lyndon Johnson whom I prefer to remember—the man who redeemed Lincoln's vision rather than the one who ruined his presidency with a needless war. He has a capacity to lead by teaching and by the force of his own character. As president, his first task will be to define the moment, as both a severe crisis and the collapse of a reigning ideology. No one but a president can do this. Leadership is more challenging when national problems are not yet critical. But great presidents always have the power of definition.

When John F. Kennedy took his oath of office on January 20, 1961, the nation was prosperous. The Cold War was more like a permanent national toothache than an acute crisis. There were increasing worries that the Russians were overcoming our scientific and military lead. Those same concerns existed in the last years of the Eisenhower administration, but had not kindled a sense of urgency or optimism.

Kennedy, however, was able to challenge a new generation by proposing that America could do better, both in its national defense and its economy, as well in the model that it offered the world. He could touch the idealism of the young with tangible projects like the Peace Corps, an idea he raised in a campaign speech at the University of Michigan on October 10, 1960. Well before he took office and many months before legislation created a Peace Corps, thousands of Americans tried to volunteer.

Kennedy was most effective as a foreign policy president, in the Cuban Missile Crisis and subsequently in the beginnings of détente. He also tried to move far-reaching social legislation that was the unfinished business of the New Deal, including federal aid to education and medical insurance for the aged. However, these efforts were almost totally stymied by conservative opposition in Congress. And on civil rights, Kennedy temporized, wanting to associate himself with the cause of the Negro, fearful of alienating the white South, concerned that the movement activists were too radical, and hoping that voluntary suasion and litigation could create gradual progress. Even his 1960 campaign promise to issue an executive order to end discrimination in federally assisted housing "with the stroke of a pen" was delayed two years while Kennedy waited to get through the 1962 midterm elections. The most urgent of unfinished business would fall to his successor.

Hell, What's the Presidency for?

Unlike Roosevelt or Kennedy, Lyndon Johnson took office with a long record of legislative mastery. In the 1950s, as perhaps the most powerful Senate majority leader in the nation's history, Johnson, a southern racial moderate and a onetime New Dealer, brokered two modest civil rights bills. To his regret, these had little enforcement power.

From literally his first day in the White House, however, Johnson vowed that he would use his office to deliver full civil rights for American Negroes. When aides cautioned him that it was too early in his presidency to risk the broad support that he still enjoyed in the wake of the Kennedy assassination, Johnson replied, "Hell, what's the presidency for?"

He had been quietly prodding the Kennedys. In May and June 1963, as chairman of President Kennedy's largely toothless Committee on Equal Employment Opportunity, Vice President Johnson repeatedly warned the president and his brother, Attorney General Robert Kennedy, that by splitting the difference between the civil rights movement and the increasingly brutal response of southern governors and sheriffs, the administration was pleasing nobody and weakening its own authority and credibility. "The whites think we're just playing politics to carry New York," he told Kennedy's aide Ted Sorensen. "The Negroes [are] suspicious that we're just doing what we got to do." And the Republicans, Johnson added, are just "sitting back, giggling," at the "civil war" in the Democratic Party and Kennedy's failure to resolve the crisis. Only after demonstrators in Birmingham were brutalized by police dogs and high-pressure fire hoses did Kennedy deliver his first major address, June 11, demanding legislation and casting the civil rights issue in moral terms. The moral language was partly at Johnson's urging.

However, in November 1963, on the eve of President Kennedy's death, the prospects did not look auspicious. The proposed civil rights legislation was bogged down in committee. Robert Kennedy's Justice Department had been largely blocked in its efforts to mediate between the nonviolent direct action by demonstrators seeking civil rights and the increasingly brutal resistance on the part of southern governors and sheriffs. Public opinion polls showed that about half the voters felt Kennedy was pushing too fast. In November 1963, as Robert Kennedy prepared to resign his office to head his brother's reelection campaign, the civil rights bill was widely considered dead unless Democrats made big congressional gains in the 1964 election.

Yet when Congress passed the landmark Civil Rights Act of 1964 the following July, it was the same Eighty-eighth Congress elected in November 1962 that had refused to move President Kennedy's legislation—the same racist southern Democratic committee chairmen, the same number of Republicans. The difference was the bravery of the civil rights movement activists on the front lines, the growing public revulsion at the brutality of the white South—but above all Johnson's leadership. The struggle in the streets was now woven into a national morality play thanks to Johnson's willingness to use presidential power and the full legal and moral authority of the White House. This leadership energized the movement on the ground, moved public opinion, and reinforced Johnson's own legendary legislative skills.

Four days after Kennedy's murder, Johnson delivered his first address to a joint session of Congress. Among his key subjects was civil rights.

> No memorial oration or eulogy could more eloquently honor President Kennedy's memory than the earliest possible passage of the civil rights bill for which he fought so long. We have talked long enough in this country about civil rights. We have talked about it for one hundred years or more. It is time now to write the next chapter, and write it into a book of law . . .
>
> . . . So let us put an end to the teaching and preaching of hate and violence. Let us turn away from the fanatics of the far left and the far right, from the apostles of bitterness and bigotry, from those defiant of law, and those who pour venom into the nation's bloodstream.

By "those defiant of law," President Johnson was referring not to Martin Luther King Jr. but to lawless southern government officials. King and his allies in the movement were euphoric. What Johnson had done, in both his public and his private words to King, was not just to press for legislation, but to encourage the movement to redouble its efforts, knowing that it had the full backing of the White House. He was deliberately increasing the pressure on himself to deliver. And then Johnson went to work on Congress and the other power brokers in town.

The civil rights bill was transformative of the apartheid regime in the South. It ended discrimination in employment, transportation, and public accommodations such as hotels, restaurants, and theaters. It added new powers to end school segregation, and provided federal enforcement of the right to vote. Not surprisingly, LBJ never won over the Dixiecrats. In a meeting on December 9, 1964, with Georgia senator Richard Russell, formerly his mentor and closest ally in the Senate, Johnson declared: "I'm not going to cavil and I'm not going to compromise. I'm going to pass it just as it is, Dick, and if you get in my way I'm going to run you down. I just wanted you to know that, because I care about you."

"Mr. President, you may be right," Russell shot back. "But if you do run me over, it will not only cost you the South, it will cost you the election."

Johnson did run over southern senators, and he did win enactment of the Civil Rights Act. Yet the scale of his subsequent election victory in November 1964 was second only to Roosevelt's in 1936. Recognizing that he would still lose the Dixiecrats, Johnson turned to the Republicans, historically the party of Lincoln. However, in 1964 as in 1864 the Grand Old Party was divided and ambivalent on how hard to push civil rights. He assiduously courted both the Republican leader in the House, Representative Charles Halleck, and the vain Republican Senate leader, Everett McKinley Dirksen, giving him ambassadorships, granting federal projects for Illinois, and stroking Dirksen's outsized ego.

By early March, Dirksen promised Johnson his support—but then he cast a vote to send the bill to Mississippi senator James Eastland's Judiciary Committee, where it would face certain burial. Civil rights activists picketed Dirksen's House. In late March, civil rights forces won a key vote on a parliamentary motion to send the bill directly to the Senate floor, bypassing Eastland. That measure got sixty votes, still seven shy of the majority necessary to break a filibuster under the rules that prevailed in the 1960s. As late as April, Dirksen was still proposing crippling amendments. Eventually, Johnson just wore him down.

But even Johnson recognized that the liberals plainly lacked the votes for the most far-reaching section. The bill's key voting rights provision would have to be excised, to be won or lost in separate legislation after the November election. Until they could vote, blacks would still be second-class citizens.

On June 10, 1964, the Senate clerk called the roll. Sixty-seven senators voted cloture to break the longest filibuster in US history.

They included Senator Clair Engle of California, dying of a brain tumor, who had to be wheeled onto the Senate floor from his hospital bed. All but six Republicans voted with Johnson.

Meanwhile, in dusty southern towns, the struggle continued, and so did the official repression. On June 21, only days after the Senate vote for passage, three civil rights workers— Chaney, Schwerner, Goodman—were kidnapped and murdered in Mississippi. The Freedom Summer effort was aimed at the one provision that even Lyndon Johnson had not managed to win, the fundamental right to register and vote.

That summer, movement activists fanned out across the South, but the segregationist power structure was not about to let Negroes vote. Things worsened in the autumn and winter.

The landslide election of November 1964 increased the Democratic margins from 66 to 68 in the Senate, and from 259 to an astounding 295 in the House, a better than two-to-one margin that nearly equaled FDR's at the peak of his power. But the right to vote continued to be denied throughout the Deep South, and when legal maneuvers failed the white power structure turned to terror. In Mississippi, just 6 percent of qualified blacks had been permitted to register. While Johnson tried to use the tools of existing law, the movement escalated its tactics.

On March 7, Dr. King began his historic march from Selma to Montgomery, Alabama, to register blacks to vote. Alabama officials were determined to block the peaceful march. On their first try, the roughly 500 marchers got just six blocks before being turned back by police batons, bull whips, tear gas, and even crude weapons fashioned from barbed wire. The police were joined by a hastily deputized mob. A white minister from Boston, the Reverend James Reeb, was killed.

America finally witnessed, on national television, the raw terrorism, stripped of its pretenses, that had maintained the system of racial privilege and oppression in the South since before the Civil War. An outpouring of national outrage followed. Thousands of people converged on Selma to join Dr. King, who would be beaten back a second time. Finally, 3,000 people would join him to complete the march, their right of peaceful assembly protected by National Guard troops placed under federal command by order of the president of the United States.

It was in this climate of the breakdown of law that Lyndon Johnson addressed Congress and the nation March 15. In just the way that FDR more than thirty years before had spelled out what had befallen the banking system, what the president was doing to remedy the crisis, and what he expected of the people, Johnson spoke masterly words about civil rights.

> At times, history and fate meet at a single time in a single place to shape a turning point in man's unending search for freedom. So it was at Lexington and Concord. So it was a century ago at Appomattox. So it was last week in Selma, Alabama. There, long-suffering men and women peacefully protested the denial of their rights as Americans. Many of them were brutally assaulted. One good man—a man of God—was killed.
>
> . . . [R]arely in any time does an issue lay bare the secret heart of America itself. Rarely are we met with a challenge, not to our growth or abundance, or our welfare or our security, but rather to the values and the purposes and the meaning of our beloved nation. The issue of equal rights for American Negroes is such an issue. And should we defeat every enemy, and should we double our wealth and conquer the stars, and still be unequal to this issue, then we will have failed as a people and as a nation . . .
>
> There is no Negro problem. There is no Southern problem. There is no Northern problem. There is only an American problem.

Johnson defined the struggle for civil rights as the essence of the American purpose. The similarity to Obama's celebrated

2004 Red State/Blue State speech is haunting. Obama, a close student of the civil rights movement, must have read this speech. Johnson was making the civil rights cause everyone's cause. Then he minced no words in explaining just what was being done to keep blacks from voting, and why we needed the strongest federal law since the military occupation of the South.

Every device of which human ingenuity is capable has been used to deny this right. The Negro citizen may go to register only to be told that the day is wrong, or the hour is late, or the official in charge is absent. And if he persists, and if he manages to present himself to the registrar, he may be disqualified because he did not spell out his middle name, or because he abbreviated a word on the application. And if he manages to fill out an application, he is given a test. The registrar is the sole judge of whether he passes this test. He may be asked to recite the entire Constitution, or explain the most complex provisions of state law.

And even a college degree cannot be used to prove that he can read and write. For the fact is that the only way to pass these barriers is to show a white skin. Experience has clearly shown that the existing process of law cannot overcome systematic and ingenious discrimination. No law that we now have on the books, and I have helped to put three of them there, can insure the right to vote when local officials are determined to deny it. In such a case, our duty must be clear to all of us. The Constitution says that no person shall be kept from voting because of his race or his color.

We have all sworn an oath before God to support and to defend that Constitution. We must now act in obedience to that oath. Wednesday, I will send to Congress a law designed to eliminate illegal barriers to the right to vote. This bill will establish a simple, uniform standard which cannot be used, however ingenious the effort, to flout our Constitution. It will provide for citizens to be registered by officials of the United States Government, if the state officials refuse to register them. It will eliminate tedious, unnecessary lawsuits which delay the right to vote.

And then, having startled his listeners with his directness, his shaming, and his moral witness, Johnson topped even that, adding slowly, calmly, and with utter determination:

But even if we pass this bill the battle will not be over. What happened in Selma is part of a far larger movement which reaches into every section and state of America. It is the effort of American Negroes to secure for themselves the full blessings of American life. Their cause must be our cause too. Because it's not just Negroes, but really it's all of us, who must overcome the crippling legacy of bigotry and injustice.

And we shall overcome.

For people who did not live through that era, it is difficult to convey the radicalism of the president of the United States, in the measured drawl of the Deep South, declaring on national television the three fraught words. "We *shall* overcome." Watching, as a college student, I literally could not believe what I had just heard. Today "We Shall Overcome" may be remembered as a folksong with political overtones, but in 1965 it was an anthem that vowed civil disobedience, a willingness to brave bodily harm, jail, and even death, to win long-deferred human rights. In adopting the anthem of the civil rights movement as his own credo, Johnson was associating himself not just with its legitimate demand for justice but with its radicalism. The immense power of the United States and the moral authority of the presidency was siding with people who were willing to break the law to enforce the Constitution.

It would be five more months before Congress finally passed the Voting Rights Act. It would take more marches, more beatings, and more of Johnson's famous "treatment" to move wavering legislators. But Johnson had won over public opinion to the proposition that the civil rights marchers had justice and the entire meaning of America on their side. In future years, right into the twenty-first century, all kinds of devious maneuvers would still to be used to block the right of blacks to vote and to have their votes counted. But never again would blacks seeking to exercise the franchise be brutalized by the state.

It may be hard, in the eighth year of the reign of George Bush II, for some readers to believe that the presidency *has* moral authority. But the history of the uses of power by Roosevelt and Lincoln and Johnson, and the fascination with the leadership potential of Barack Obama, suggest that the latent authority of the president of the United States to appeal to our best selves has not been extinguished, only anesthetized. Some may think that after eight years of Bush, Americans are fearful of presidential leadership per se. But political scientists distinguish between power and authority. Power can be brute force. Authority is earned respect. The fear of abusive presidential power is the flip side of a hunger for legitimate authority that only great leadership can restore.

Lyndon Johnson's use of the moral power of the presidency holds one other lesson for Obama. Sometimes it is not enough to appeal to national unity and all of the common yearnings that unite us as Americans. Johnson surely did that in his voting rights address. He appealed both to our highest principles as a people and to our collective sense of shame. But this was also a contest between good and evil, and Johnson did not shrink from using the full powers of the White House to obliterate the capacity of the evildoers to block full civil rights.

When he was a young schoolteacher in Southwest Texas, he recalled in that magnificent speech, he had watched the despair on the faces of his Mexican American pupils.

And somehow you never forget what poverty and hatred can do when you see its scars on the hopeful face of a young child.

I never thought then, in 1928, that I would be standing here in 1965. It never even occurred to me in my fondest dreams that I might have the chance to help the sons and daughters of those students, and to help people like them all over this country. But now I do have that chance.

And I'll let you in on a secret—I mean to use it.

By the same token, Roosevelt often appealed to the unity and the common purpose of the nation, but there were times when he needed to name the forces that were blocking reform. Announcing a Second New Deal on October 31, 1936, on the eve of an election that would be American history's greatest vindication, Roosevelt looked back on the triumphs of his first term and declared,

> We had to struggle with the old enemies of peace—business and financial monopoly, speculation, reckless banking, class antagonism, sectionalism, war profiteering.
>
> They had begun to consider the Government of the United States as a mere appendage to their own affairs. We know now that Government by organized money is just as dangerous as Government by organized mob.
>
> Never before in all our history have these forces been so united against one candidate as they stand today. They are unanimous in their hate for me—and I welcome their hatred.

Missing the Wave

A crisis, in the well-known Chinese formulation, is also an opportunity. But not every president who faces a crisis rises to the occasion. The Great Depression festered for more than three years while Herbert Hoover failed to deliver either hope or help. Jimmy Carter took office with great popular goodwill after the trauma of Nixon era, as well as overwhelming Democratic majorities in both Houses of Congress. But when twin crises of energy and stagflation hit, he failed to deal with either.

Carter came to Washington as the ultimate outsider. He served just one term as governor of Georgia; and after he left office in January 1975, he spent the next twenty-two months running for president. At the time I was working on *The Washington Post* as the junior man on the paper's national staff. When Carter formally declared for president in a speech that spring at the National Press Club, I drew the assignment. So unlikely a candidate was Carter that hardly any other reporters showed up, and the *Post* put my story on the shipping page.

He began with just 2-percent national name recognition. But Carter had the fortune to run in a year when the voters were fed up with Washington and welcomed a complete outsider candidate. Like other outsiders, Carter also ran against Congress. But unlike successful presidents, he failed to build bridges to the congressional leadership once he assumed office. His two top aides, the late Hamilton Jordan and his press secretary Jody Powell, were both somewhat provincial and disdainful of Congress—and Congress returned the favor. Jordan, who pronounced his name *Jerdan,* was famous for telling new acquaintances, "My friends call me Jerdan, but you can call me Jordan." That may have had them rolling in the aisles in Atlanta, but it didn't amuse House Speaker Tip O'Neill.

The Speaker, who hated Reagan's policies but nonetheless enjoyed a cordial relationship with the engaging Gipper, didn't care for the whole Carter crowd. He referred to Carter's quirky chief of staff as "Hannibal Jerkin."

During the Carter presidency, unemployment and inflation rose in tandem, triggered by the aftereffects of the first OPEC oil price shock in 1973. Carter never managed to develop an effective anti-inflation policy. His Treasury secretary and then Federal

Reserve chairman, G. William Miller, was considered largely ineffectual in a crisis. Carter replaced him with Paul Volcker, then the president of the Federal Reserve Bank of New York, an inflation hawk. Eventually, Volcker tamed inflation by raising interest rates to a peak of more than 20 percent—in the thick of Carter's reelection campaign.

Nor did Carter manage to broker an adequate energy policy. He tried to promote conservation by example, turning down the thermostats at the White House and in other government buildings, wearing cardigan sweaters, and installing solar panels and a woodstove at the White House. He also deregulated energy prices, launched a program to develop synthetic fuels, and successfully legislated fuel-efficiency standards. But in an era of soaring oil prices and long lines at gas pumps, it did not add up to a policy.

In fairness, transforming America's energy consumption would have been a Herculean feat for any president. But Carter lacked two core qualifications. He never mastered the art of either inspiring the people or working with Congress. Carter was a man of abiding principle, idealism, and morality. Those qualities shone through in his post-presidency. However, as president, his attempts to appeal to ethical norms often sounded merely reproachful or preachy. His high purpose was not enough.

At the peak of the energy crisis, Carter gave his famous "malaise" speech, which never actually used the word *malaise*. Carter had heard from his pollsters that citizens were suffering from a loss of confidence. He had confirmed that conclusion firsthand, in a listening tour.

"I want to speak to you first tonight about a subject even more serious than energy or inflation," he began his speech of July 15, 1979. "I want to talk to you right now about a fundamental threat to American democracy. The threat is nearly invisible in ordinary ways. It is a crisis of confidence. It is a crisis that strikes at the very heart and soul and spirit of our national will. We can see this crisis in the growing doubt about the meaning of our own lives and in the loss of a unity of purpose for our nation."

The speech aspired to be Rooseveltian and was genuinely eloquent in places. But many commentators felt that the president was trying to deflect blame for failed policies onto the people. Voters were less worried about "the meaning of their own lives" than the price of oil. Three days later, in a moment of despair and pique, Carter asked for the resignation of his entire cabinet, a move calculated to suggest a fresh start but one that conveyed bewilderment and panic.

He was both the most anti-party Democrat in a century and the most Republican of Democratic presidents in his policy views since Grover Cleveland. He fled from the New Deal/Great Society philosophy and embraced a number of conservative ideas—deregulation of industry after industry, tax cuts on the upper brackets, privatization. When Reagan took office in 1981, Carter had softened the ground.

Professor Burns wrote of Carter:

> His Administration attested not so much to political or administrative incompetence as to a collapse of political strategy stemming largely from a failure of intellectual leadership . . . He wanted to be a teaching president . . . a preaching president. . . Beyond platitudes about honesty and morality, however, and specific policies the president was interested in at the moment, it was not clear that this transcending leadership was *for*. Tragically for Carter's presidency, the one vehicle that might have helped shape and support a coherent program—the Democratic Party—was the one he most neglected.

Fatal Triangles

Bill Clinton is remembered as a far more successful president than Jimmy Carter. The economy thrived on his watch (though some of the prosperity was built on unsustainable bubbles). His foreign policy was competent and occasionally inspired, as in the Camp David Accords and in the Kosovo settlement. He presided over fiscal discipline and reform of government agencies. His appointments were generally first-rate. But he failed to defend or advance his party's principles, leaving voters skeptical of government and reinforcing Republican ideology. His signature was "triangulation"—splitting the difference, simulating leadership often at the expense of his own party.

Like Lincoln, Roosevelt, and Johnson, great presidents are sometimes defined by great enemies—and do not shrink from engaging them. In this respect, one key reason why Clinton could not win enactment of his health program was his failure to make good use of the near-perfect enemy that history had offered him—the health insurance industry. It was an era when the line "Goddamn HMO" in a popular movie shortly afterward would elicit spontaneous audience boos. Instead, Clinton hoped that the industry could be co-opted by his plan to run his new universal insurance system through private insurance companies. He also hoped he could enlist other large corporations with the prospect of capping their own premium costs.

But in the end, both the entire insurance industry and all large employers were ideologically united against giving government the power to establish a new program of social insurance that might bond voters to the Democratic Party. When Clinton tried compromise, business followed the Republicans' advice to oppose the program "sight unseen," in the phrase of strategist William Kristol. Clinton failed to pursue the one strategy that might have worked—defining a campaign of the American people against the selfish private interests.

By the same token, Clinton's success in transforming the welfare system shows how a leader can sometimes lose by winning. Clinton's original plan was one part tough love and one part expanded resources. Able long-term welfare recipients would be compelled to work, but additional resources for job training, wage subsidy, and child care, as well as waivers in hardship cases, would make welfare reform an improvement in the lives of the poor, not just a cruel reduction in benefits. But the Republican majority in Congress was more interested in cutting the rolls. Clinton vetoed the proposed legislation twice before finally signing it based on only token improvements. His secretary of health and human services, Donna Shalala, urged him to veto the bill. Three of his subcabinet officials—the designers of his reform plan—resigned in protest, a principled act almost unknown in recent times.

For Democrats as well as Republicans, the proof of success became the dramatic shrinkage of the welfare rolls, and not the more troubling question of how many of the poor were better or worse off. By embracing an essentially Republican version of welfare reform, Clinton reinforced conservative dogma that the welfare state was more of a problem than a solution. Except for his expansion of the Earned Income Tax Credit, he colluded in a net reduction of resources going to the needy, and passed up an opportunity to truly convert welfare into work support. The worsening income share of the bottom fifth of the population in the years since Clinton and the Republicans ended "welfare as we know it" is in part the result of former welfare recipients being pushed into a low-wage labor market with few offsetting supports. Clinton made a calculated decision to "take welfare off the table" as an issue that was sometimes used against Democrats. But in terms of the effect on the prevailing ideology and the treatment of the working poor, the issue went directly from the table into the bag of Republican victories.

All transformative reforms involve struggles. Forces that have resisted reform are, by definition, immensely powerful. Reform entails mobilizing the less powerful, sometimes lending presidential authority to a brave minority, as Lincoln and Roosevelt did; and sometimes building support among the people almost from scratch. The great presidents knew how to use words to inspire—but they also knew how to play hardball. Sometimes presidents get things backward. In Clinton's case, the "interest group" that he defeated was welfare recipients. The one that defeated him was the health insurance industry.

More than a quarter century ago, in his magisterial political-science study *Leadership,* James MacGregor Burns thoroughly demolished the idea that leadership is merely the art of compromise. Rather, the act of compromise is what you do, as necessary, in the endgame. But if you split the difference with your opponents going in, you are finished. "Leaders," Burns wrote, "whatever their professions of harmony, do not shun conflict; they confront it, exploit it, ultimately embody it."

Presidents at War

Not surprisingly, war and peace offer some of history's most telling successes and failures of presidential leadership. It is beyond the scope of this brief essay and my depth as a historian to add much to what biographers have already told us about Abraham Lincoln, our greatest wartime president. However, two insights, neither original to me, are worth keeping in mind as we contemplate an Obama presidency.

First, Lincoln's great challenge as president was not just to preserve the Union, or even to free the slaves. It was to win over public sentiment among what today would be called opinion leaders and the people generally. Lincoln gradually transformed how different segments of society thought about the problem of slavery, the challenge of rebuilding the Union, and the role of government in reconstruction and economic development. Out of impossible disunity, he built something close to national consensus.

After not quite a century and a half, the popular conception of Lincoln is of the president who saved the Union and freed the slaves. Often overlooked is the fact that holding together the *North* was almost as difficult a task as conquering and then reintegrating the South. "A house divided against itself cannot stand," Lincoln had warned in 1858, paraphrasing scripture. But in the war years, a divided house was a fitting description not just of the sundered Union, but of the fractious North as well. Loyalists to the Union included Radical Republicans who wanted both immediate liberation of the slaves and severe punishment of the South; War Democrats who favored a much more gradualist approach; Peace Democrats or "Copperheads" who were ready to abandon the slaves in exchange for a negotiated peace; and citizens of border states, who had narrowly opted to stay with the Union but wanted to keep their slaves.

Second, what enabled Lincoln to hold this coalition together and move it toward a viable national policy had everything to do with Lincoln's character. "Malice toward none" was not just a felicitous phrase for how Lincoln hoped to treat the conquered and ravaged South. It was how he conducted his daily human relations and mastered politics.

Lincoln's "team of rivals" included all but the most extreme representatives of these diverse factions. The cabinet was a hothouse of intrigue. Lincoln held it together with exceptional courtesy and respect, and a capacity to lead by example and by teaching. What made people his allies and admirers was not just his keen intellect and good humor. More importantly, it was his kindness, decency, idealism, and honor. He went out of his way to let people know that they were valued when he might have chosen to humiliate them. This trait reflected not just the imperatives of the time—he could not afford to sacrifice even a single potential ally—but also his abiding sense of how one treated people.

Lincoln took office pledging not to interfere with slavery in the South. After full civil war was a fact, Lincoln moved slowly and deliberately toward a decision to emancipate the slaves in the states at war with the Union, a proclamation that he issued on New Year's Day 1863. But first he took great care to consolidate both public opinion and the diverse opinions in his own cabinet. Lincoln wrote later, "It is my conviction that, had the proclamation been issued even six months earlier than it was, public sentiment would not have sustained it."

Having heartened radicals with his Emancipation Proclamation, he then set about reassuring conservatives with a plan to restore full constitutional and property rights in former rebel states once 10 percent of voters had taken an oath to support the United States. This idea infuriated many Republicans, who had hoped that rebel states would be governed as conquered territories. For good measure, Lincoln vetoed a punitive reconstruction bill sent him by Congress. Meanwhile, the Emancipation Proclamation was denounced by Democratic governors throughout the North outside abolitionist New England. So-called Peace Democrats were prepared to support a civil war to restore the Union, but not to free the slaves. But informed opinion, as reflected in newspaper editorials, speeches by notables, and ultimately in the 1864 elections, slowly shifted to Lincoln's side.

Some would say Lincoln had to reckon with Radical Republicans to his "left" and conciliatory Peace Democrats to his "right," but to credit Lincoln's leadership to his "centrism" utterly misses the essence both of Lincoln and of leadership. Had advisers like Clinton's triangulators Dick Morris or Mark Penn been counseling Lincoln, we might still have slavery, though perhaps with some labor standards.

Public opinion is widely assumed to be a twentieth-century concept, but Lincoln was among the most astute students of the public pulse ever to occupy the White House. "As a politician," writes Goodwin, "he had an intuitive sense of when to hold fast, when to wait, and when to lead." Lincoln exchanged letters with many hundreds of correspondents. He received the common people at the executive mansion. He repeatedly left the White House to speak with ordinary Americans, and made many trips to the front to engage soldiers, exploring the camps, sitting in hospital tents with the wounded, talking and listening. He issued presidential pardons to exhausted young men who had fallen asleep on sentry duty, who otherwise would have been executed. He had far more unscripted contact with regular Americans than any modern president with the possible exception of Roosevelt.

And in both his public speeches and letters, and his private dealings with his cabinet and staff, Lincoln had an exceptional gift for appealing to what was noblest in the American character— "the better angels of our nature," as he famously said in his first inaugural. Perhaps his greatest strength was his personal generosity. He had a stunning capacity to turn adversaries first into allies, then into admirers. When Treasury Secretary Salmon Chase crossed Lincoln one time too often over a patronage appointee useful for Chase's presidential aspirations, Chase issued one of many letters of resignation that Lincoln had previously rejected. This time Lincoln had had enough. In accepting the resignation, however, Lincoln promptly appointed Chase as Chief Justice of the Supreme Court.

In the four years of the Civil War, support for Lincoln gradually deepened as he won the trust of the nation. In broadening and deepening his coalition, both inside his own cabinet and in the esteem of the people, Lincoln held firmly to his principles. In due course, he believed, the slaves would be freed, given education and land; educated blacks and those who had fought in the Union army would be given the right to vote. But there would be no wholesale punishment or long-term military occupation of the South.

After his second inauguration, among those listening to Lincoln explain his plans for extending voting rights to the newly freed slaves, in a speech from the White House balcony on April 11, 1865, was John Wilkes Booth. An enraged Booth swore to "put him through," which Booth did just three days later. Had Lincoln lived, carrying out this generous policy to both the defeated white South and the newly freed slaves would have been as difficult in its own way as winning the Civil War.

The political scientist Richard Valelly, in his book *The Two Reconstructions*, poses the question: Why did the creation of black voting rights and biracial politics prove short-lived in the post–Civil War era of Reconstruction but durable in the "Second Reconstruction" of Lyndon Johnson? For a generation after the war, blacks held major office throughout the South, but by 1901 their rights had been wiped away. Biracial social movements of economic populism collapsed under a reign of fear in which the southern planter class regained much of its lost power. Valelly's is a brilliant exposition of the fragility of biracial coalition politics and the dynamics of race and social class. But one major explanation for why civil rights endured in the 1960s and collapsed after Lincoln's assassination in the 1860s was the presence or absence of presidential leadership.

It is instructive to compare Lincoln's brand of leadership with that of Roosevelt and Johnson. FDR may indeed have had a first-rate temperament, as Oliver Wendell Holmes Jr. said, but on occasion he could humiliate both subordinates and allies, and he took an almost childish delight in springing surprises on his cabinet and in playing off one aide against another. Yet, like Lincoln, he won broad admiration for his seriousness in tying his project of national recovery to the higher purposes of the nation. Johnson, with his legislative cunning, had yet another approach to cobbling together majorities and winning over public opinion. What all three had in common was a deep and sincere faith in America's highest principles.

The point is not that a president like Obama needs to copy this or that trait of Lincoln, Roosevelt, or Johnson. It is that he needs to reach for what is most brave and honorable in his own character.

Preparing a Nation for War

Our other great wartime president was Franklin Roosevelt. He is known both for his leadership of the Allied victory over the Axis and his remarkable success on the home front, where America was mobilized to produce nearly 300,000 warplanes, more than 2 million military trucks, and over 100,000 tanks in less than five years. During the war, wage and price controls prevented inflation without strangling business, which enjoyed profitability. There was no compulsory labor and no nationalization of industry, yet there was total mobilization. As Goodwin writes, "Roosevelt's success in mobilizing the nation to this extraordinary level of collective performance rested on his uncanny sensitivity to his followers, his ability to appraise public feeling and lead the people one step at a time."

Yet if anything, Roosevelt's more impressive act of leadership was preparing the nation for war. Like Winston Churchill, Roosevelt perceived long before shooting broke out that another war was very likely and that his country was woefully unprepared. With modern long-range aircraft, Roosevelt kept warning, the United States could suffer attack on its home soil. But America in late 1930s was in a mood of profound isolationism. Meanwhile, Hitler and Mussolini in Europe and Tojo in Asia were pursuing their plans of territorial annexation largely unmolested. As Roosevelt repeatedly said, he viewed these men as mere gangsters who happened to hold state power.

As early as October 1937, even before the Munich capitulation, Roosevelt gave a tough foreign policy speech in Chicago, one that came as a total surprise to his foreign policy aides. The very foundations of civilization and international order were at stake, he warned, as dictators violated treaty commitments with impunity. And if war came, the Western Hemisphere could not avoid attack. "The peace-loving nations must make a concerted effort in opposition to those violations of treaties and those ignorings of humane instincts which today are creating a state of international anarchy and instability from which there is no escape through mere isolation or neutrality." Then he added a medical metaphor. "When an epidemic of physical disease starts to spread, the community approves and joins in a quarantine."

In effect, Roosevelt was repudiating the foundation of inter-war American foreign policy, the Neutrality Act. And he was doing so without consulting either his secretary of state or the Democratic leaders in Congress, all of whom would have advised against it. Back in Washington, the response was chilly. His own party leaders did not rally to his defense, and the Republicans jumped all over him. "It is a terrible thing," Roosevelt later told his close counselor Sam Rosenman, "to look over your shoulder when you are trying to lead—and to find no one there."

While he was compelled to pull back for the moment, just as Lincoln kept deferring emancipation of the slaves, Roosevelt did not give up. Turning around isolationist America would take three more years. He moved, step by step, delivering very bold and risky speeches to move public opinion, initiating policies sometimes by executive action and sometimes with the collaboration of Congress, and occasionally making tactical retreats.

In June and July 1939, Congress refused to go along with Roosevelt's request to repeal the arms embargo provisions of the Neutrality Act. Even after Hitler invaded Poland on September 1, 1939, and Hitler was officially at war with Britain and France, US public opinion remained ambivalent. A Gallup poll showed that 84 percent of respondents hoped for an Allied victory, with only 2 percent favoring the Nazis; yet only 37 percent of Americans favored helping France and Britain.

Roosevelt then hit on the tactic of using isolationist sentiment to build support for aiding the democracies that were the front lines of battle against Hitler. If America could help them keep the dictators at bay, war could be kept from America's shores. This became the theme of Roosevelt's speeches and messages to Congress, and it suggests the presidential power to move public opinion.

On May 16, 1940, a week after Hitler ended the "Phony War" with a blitzkrieg invasion of Belgium, Holland, Luxembourg, and parts of France, Roosevelt addressed a joint session of Congress and called for massive rearmament. In June, he added two leading pro-intervention senior Republicans to his cabinet: Frank Knox, who had been Landon's running mate in 1936, as secretary of the navy; and Henry Stimson, a leading Republican internationalist, as secretary of war. But Congress was still balking.

With Paris under Nazi occupation by mid-June and German bombing of southern England having begun in July, a vulnerable

Britain was expecting an invasion any day. Winston Churchill cabled Roosevelt that with the English Channel underdefended, what he most needed were at least fifty destroyers. But US law still provided that ships could be sold only if not needed for the America's own national defense, and then only with congressional approval.

It was Navy Secretary Knox who proposed the idea Roosevelt would use. The United States would not sell Britain the destroyers. Rather, we would barter the destroyers in exchange for a ninety-nine-year lease of British bases in the Western Hemisphere. This plan, a thin fig leaf, technically did not need the approval of Congress.

Roosevelt announced the deal September 3, on the eve of his unprecedented run for a third term. All hell broke loose. Republican candidate Wendell Willkie denounced the president's end run around Congress as "the most dictatorial and arbitrary of any President in the history of the US." The isolationist press was furious. As Burns wrote, "For Roosevelt, the destroyer deal was a colossal political risk. He told friends that he might lose the election on the issue. Even more, if England should fall and the Nazis gain control of the British fleet, the President would be fair game for the Republicans, for in that event the fifty destroyers would be turned against their former owners . . . Not only had Roosevelt dared to act—he had acted without Congress."

But in Berlin, where on the same day, September 3, the Nazi high command had distributed operational orders for the invasion of Britain, the move may have had a different impact. America was now effectively allied with Britain. Hitler temporized. He kept delaying the date; in mid-October, the invasion was put off until spring. By then, Britain was better defended, and invasion never came.

More than a year before Pearl Harbor, the United States was now decisively allied against the dictators, and committed to accelerated war preparations. Along with the destroyer deal came Roosevelt's campaign for an unprecedented peacetime draft.

After Roosevelt put all his prestige and powers of persuasion on the line, the House of Representatives approved the Selective Service Act, by a single vote—another huge risk on the eve of an election. The first draftees reported for duty in October 1940, giving America a crucial fourteen months to build up its forces before the Japanese attack came.

There followed a gradual, then massive, increase in appropriations for American rearmament and supply of the nations fighting Hitler, first with congressional reluctance, then with enthusiasm. During this period, Roosevelt gave speech after speech making the case, as he famously put it in a Fireside Chat on December 29, 1940, that the United States needed to be the "arsenal of democracy." Said Roosevelt,

> The Nazi masters of Germany have made it clear that they intend not only to dominate all life and thought in their own country, but also to enslave the whole of Europe, and then to use the resources of Europe to dominate the rest of the world . . . If Great Britain goes down, the Axis powers will control the continents of Europe, Asia, Africa, Australia, and the high seas—and they will be in a position to bring enormous military and naval resources against this hemisphere. It is no exaggeration to say that all of us, in all the Americas, would be living at the point of a gun—a gun loaded with explosive bullets, economic as well as military.

Only in March 1941 did Congress pass legislation, 260 to 165 in the House and 60 to 31 in the Senate, formalizing and dramatically expanding the Lend-Lease Program of arms shipments to the Allies. The bill was passed after six weeks of congressional and national debate, during which time a divided public gradually shifted to supporting the bill by a margin of almost two to one. Speaking at the White House Correspondents Dinner on March 15, after signing the act, Roosevelt declared,

We have just now engaged in a great debate. It was not limited to the halls of Congress. It was argued in every newspaper, on every wave length, over every cracker barrel in all the land; and it was finally settled and decided by the American people themselves.

Yes, the decisions of our democracy may be slowly arrived at. But when that decision is made, it is proclaimed not with the voice of any one man but with the voice of 130 millions.

By the time Pearl Harbor was attacked, Roosevelt had transformed American public opinion and defeated isolationism. The American military was ready, though just barely. But the American people were ready.

Fear Itself

The comparison with George W. Bush's push for war against Iraq is revealing, on several counts. Like Roosevelt, Bush endeavored to educate the American people, to persuade Congress to either approve or stand aside, and sometimes to ignore Congress entirely. But unlike Roosevelt, whose worst sin was a borderline legal fiction as cover for the destroyer deal—Bush's war was based on actual fictions on the ground and knowing misrepresentations as well as self-deceptions. Nor was the Iraq War a true "decision of our democracy," in Roosevelt's phrase, for the country remained bitterly divided as well as manipulated by fear and snookered by doctored evidence.

Roosevelt also had immense respect for American and British intelligence professionals. One reason that the D-Day invasion succeeded against immense tactical odds was that US and British intelligence of German troop movements and defense plans was superb. Roosevelt and his commander, General Eisenhower, repeatedly altered the location and the timing of the Normandy invasion in response to intelligence findings. By contrast, when Bush and Cheney did not like the intelligence reports they received, they fired the messenger and made up their own intelligence.

After 9/11, in asking congressional approval for his invasion of Afghanistan to defeat the Taliban, Bush enjoyed almost universal support. Had he used the aftermath of 9/11 to promote national unity, shared sacrifice, and the constructive use of government, Bush might have been one of America's great presidents. In the end, Bush failed either to win over public opinion or to realize his grand design for the export of American democracy to the Middle East, because his premises were so unreal. His defenders even turned their fantasies into a virtue, mocking Bush's critics as "reality-based."

According to Robert Schlesinger's recent book on presidential ghostwriting, one of Bush's speechwriters, David Frum, charged with writing a draft speech justifying the Iraq War, consulted several of Roosevelt's great speeches. Frum, according to Schlesinger, noticed how FDR repeatedly mentioned the multiple menace of the Axis powers—Hitler, Mussolini, and Tojo. This was the inspiration for Frum/Bush's declaration that Iraq, Iran, and North Korea were an "axis of evil." The only problem was that the World War II Axis was a genuine military alliance; Iran and Iraq were enemies, while North Korea has little connection with either. Bush's Axis, unlike Roosevelt's, was a fiction.

If Roosevelt's credo was "The only thing we have to fear is fear itself," Bush's might have been, "The only thing we have to use is fear itself." The continually changing color-coded alerts that frightened Americans on the eve of the 2004 election faded to static orange when they were no longer politically useful.

Yet, however trumped-up, crisis served Bush's goal of enlarged presidential power. Time after time, Bush expanded presidential powers based on invented doctrines, and he often intimidated Congress into going along, playing on the anxieties of Democrats who feared being painted as unsupportive of national security. As late as July 2008, with Bush's popularity close to its all-time low, *The New York Times* could publish a front-page story:

SENATE APPROVES BILL TO BROADEN WIRETAP POWERS
ANOTHER BUSH VICTORY
69–28 VOTE—TELECOM COMPANIES GRANTED LEGAL IMMUNITY

As Obama eloquently pointed out in his address of July 15, 2008, the opportunity to build genuine national unity after the all-too-real attack of 9/11 was sacrificed to the cynical use of the attacks to move a far-right agenda that never enjoyed majority support. Belatedly, the people noticed the fakery. As the great political scientist V. O. Key Jr. once put it, "The voters are not fools." But how much sooner they might have noticed the fakery had there been braver leadership on the Democratic side.

Among the bravest was Obama, in a risky speech delivered at an antiwar rally in Chicago in late October 2002, when he was a political unknown just beginning to consider a campaign for the US Senate. "I don't oppose all wars," he began.

> What I am opposed to is a dumb war. What I am opposed to is a rash war. What I am opposed to is the cynical attempt by Richard Perle, Paul Wolfowitz and other armchair, weekend warriors to shove their own ideological agendas down our throats, irrespective of the costs in lives lost and hardships borne. What I am opposed to is the attempt by political hacks like Karl Rove to distract us from a rise in the uninsured, a rise in the poverty rate, a drop on the median income—to distract us from the corporate scandals . . .

That was six years ago, less than a year after 9/11. Not bad for a post-partisan. Not bad for connecting the dots. Not bad for prescience and courage.

Leadership and Partnership

As the Bush presidency sputters to an end, there are paradoxical implications for the challenge of leadership. For nearly half a century, since James MacGregor Burns described Congress's blockage of John Kennedy's agenda as a "Deadlock of Democracy," the pendulum has swung back and forth between an overly imperial presidency and one held captive by Congress. No sooner had Burns's book been published than Lyndon Johnson persuaded Congress to enact most of Kennedy's stalled agenda and then some. But almost immediately afterward, Johnson was humbled by popular and Senate opposition to his war, and he stunned America by abdicating. Nixon's story was a more extreme version of Johnson's—presidential hubris, brought to justice by a vigilant press and a resurgent Congress. The pendulum swings back and forth, through the weak presidency of Carter, the strong one of Reagan, the triangulated one of Clinton, the autocratic one of Bush.

The power of Congress also ebbed and flowed as Congress ended funding for the Vietnam War, reined in the spying abuses of the Cold War, impeached Nixon, co-opted Clinton—but then proved itself putty in the hands of George W. Bush, a man who never had much of a real mandate or more than a very narrow margin in Congress, but who took more liberties with the Constitution and the truth than any previous president. The slight figure who play-acted the role of imperious chief executive was actually the pawn of his vice president, another first in American history.

The paradox for 2009 is that America needs both a restoration of constitutional government *and* strong presidential leadership to surmount a severe economic crisis and to break the shackles of conventional assumptions about what government can and should do. But this paradox is hardly a contradiction when one reviews the achievements of great leaders. As Doris Kearns Goodwin writes, in the preface to her remarkable study of Lincoln's leadership, "In the hands of a truly great politician the qualities we generally associate with decency and morality— kindness, sensitivity, compassion, honesty, and empathy—can also be impressive political resources."

For Barack Obama, the moral is that the presidency offers extraordinary, often untapped, opportunities for leadership; that an eloquent and principled president has immense power to define the moment and transform the nation. The secret ingre- dient of lasting presidential leadership is character. The public hungers for such leadership. Congress can either be pounded into submission or cultivated as a partner. But if success is to be dura- ble, presidential leadership had better be rooted in reality.

Today the reality is of deepening economic crisis, overlaid on thirty years of diminishing economic security for most Americans. It is a reality to which most politician pay lip service, but too few are prepared to redress. The crisis needs to be named before it can be tamed. Here, as we shall see in chapters 3 and 4, is Obama's greatest challenge.

three

Audacity Versus Undertow

There go my people, I must find out where they are going
so I can lead them.
— ALEXANDRE AUGUSTE LEDRU-ROLLIN,
Paris, circa 1789

Worldly wisdom teaches us that it is better for reputation to
fail conventionally than to succeed unconventionally.
— JOHN MAYNARD KEYNES, 1936

Which sort of leader will Obama be? The past year has brought financial collapse, but not yet a collapse of the ideology and the habits of mind that produced the crisis. Connecting those dots will be Obama's first challenge.

As I write these words, the mortgage giants Fannie Mae and Freddie Mac have just been bailed out by Congress, and more banks are failing. Regulatory policy hovers between two treacherous stools of abdication and bailout—inviting windfall private gains while leaving the taxpayers on the hook for the risks. Treasury Secretary Henry Paulson, a champion of further deregulation, is frantically promoting government rescue plans that entail the most interventionist policies since Roosevelt, but without acknowledging the 180-degree philosophical reversal. As America witnessed the first runs on big banks since the 1930s, George W. Bush, one of the greatest government-bashers ever, rather pathetically reassured depositors: "My hope is that people take a deep breath and realize that their deposits are protected by the government." Imagine that.

Obama needs to interpret what has befallen the economy, both to slay the failed ideology and to lead a recovery based on a far more robust use of government. However, he faces a potent conservative undertow, as least as strong as the one that confounded Roosevelt during the 1932 campaign and in his first weeks in office.

Like Roosevelt, Obama is constrained by a fiscal climate of opinion in which right-thinking people are supposed to be more alarmed about budgetary threats than about either the risks of another depression or a continued slow decline in the economic security and opportunity of most Americans. Regulation is still widely considered a pejorative word. Obama also must hose away a prevailing ideology in which large government endeavors are deemed to be outmoded by modern markets, politically risky, as well as fiscally moot—and then rebuild a progressive ideology to inform and animate a recovery program. He inherits a large stable of Democratic pollsters and campaign operatives, many of whom do nothing so much as reinforce the disabling conventional wisdom.

Here is the frame that needs to be broken. It is a frame tacitly accepted by a majority of voters—not because they like it but because it has been a very long time since any effective national leader has offered them a credible alternative. The frame is beginning to crack, but the consensus alternative is still too feeble to repair the economy.

1. The fiscal cupboard is bare.
2. Government is generally perverse or incompetent.
3. Tax cuts are one of the few benefits that governments can reliably deliver.
4. Private markets invariably work better than government.

And the political corollary:

5. Successful Democrats need to talk more like
Republicans.

Conservative opinion leaders repeat these claims ad nauseam, creating a climate of conventional belief; and then even moderately liberal politicians repeat what they think the public wants to hear, thus reinforcing the supposed iron consensus. When poll after poll shows that the voters actually want government to do more, the results are dismissed as anomalies. Let's take these one at a time.

1. The fiscal cupboard is bare.

In recent years, the view that government faces a crisis of dangerously large current deficits, as well as runaway long-term entitlements, has pervaded the political spectrum. Commentators have confused two sets of entirely distinct debates and then muddled the issues into one blurred, all-purpose rant against public spending.

The first set of issues to be disentangled are these: How big a government do we need? What do we need it to do? How shall we pay for it? And how large a deficit is prudent?

Each of these is a distinct question. It may be that a federal government that spends 20 percent (roughly the current share) of GDP is sufficient, especially if we reject adventures like the Iraq War and shift the money to rebuilding the economy. Or it may be that economic recovery and the restoration of broadly shared prosperity requires the federal government to spend more like 25 percent of GDP collectively.

Further, we can have a balanced budget, a moderate deficit, or an irresponsibly large deficit, at any level of public outlay. The relative size of the deficit is an entirely separate question from how much of GDP we spend through the public sector, and what we spend it on. Reagan and both Presidents Bush, for example, increased the deficit while they reduced nonmilitary government outlays.

Unfortunately, ever since Ross Perot began howling about it, deficit reduction has become a general proxy for public virtue; politicians all across the spectrum feel the need to honor the conventional wisdom, which is repeated endlessly by commentators professing to be ideologically neutral. In fact, the holy grail of smaller government and budget balance is deeply conservative, as Roosevelt found when he tried to out-Hoover Hoover.

A second layer of deficit issues concerns the supposed entitlement crisis. Here again, several separate questions have been deliberately entangled, often by people opposed to the whole idea of social insurance, who paint as bleak a picture as possible. They are joined by well-meaning souls who think they are being responsible "to future generations."

In the case of Medicare, there really is a fiscal crisis. But Medicare's budget problems can't be solved except as part of universal health reform. Health costs are inflating far faster than personal incomes because we have such an inefficient system. Medicare cannot function efficiently as an island of social medicine in an ocean of wasteful and fragmented for-profit health insurance.

Absent true reform of the way we organize the health system, the present course involves ever-deeper cuts in Medicare outlays, which translate into reduced payments to doctors and reduced services to patients. The supposed reforms would achieve the same kinds of cuts via a more systematic route—Medicare payments would be explicitly capped or turned into a voucher. The non-rich citizen would exchange the voucher for even less adequate insurance, and middlemen would take out even more in fees and profits. Leadership is required to explain that only national health insurance simultaneously solves the triple problems of cost, coverage, and security. The American people would support that, but Obama is not there yet.

In the case of Social Security, the crisis is mostly fake. The rather dour projections of the Social Security Trustees, which have been proven overly pessimistic for the past decade, forecast a seventy-five-year shortfall in the Social Security trust funds of less than 1 percent of GDP. The Congressional Budget Office, with more realistic assumptions, projects the deficit at about one-third of 1 percent. The supposed shortfall is within the statistical margin of error. And if the birthrate of the children of immigrants continues rising, or if the long-term economic growth rate is better than the dismal 1.4-percent premise that the trustees have used after 2010, the imbalance disappears entirely.

The real crisis is one of inadequate retirement income—the result of large corporations getting out of the business of providing secure pensions. Devices such as 401(k) plans are tax-sheltered savings schemes; they are not true pensions. There are several good strategies for restoring acceptable retirement income, but all of them require far more active government policies. The best would be a second tier of Social Security, with tax-supported, fully portable accounts funded in advance.

However, the supposed crisis of Social Security has tripped up even our most astute liberal politicians. In May 2007, Obama accepted the premise that Social Security suffered from a mighty shortfall. Seeking to establish himself as a politician not afraid to tackle hard issues, Obama declared his support for raising the cap on income subject to Social Security taxation (currently $102,000) and chided Senator Clinton for not doing likewise. Obama at first implied that in his administration, everything would be on the table—higher taxes, lower benefits. He later explained that he would increase taxes only on people making $250,000 or over, and that he would not reduce benefits. But Obama needlessly accepted conservative conventional wisdom, and then set a trap for himself in having to remedy a false crisis.

Why did Obama fall into this trap? Here is a sampler of the kind of supposedly high-minded thinking that pervades Washington and the media.

Peter G. Peterson, the onetime secretary of commerce under Richard Nixon and billionaire former partner of the Blackstone Group, a private equity firm, has written four books over the past two decades bemoaning the cost of entitlements and forecasting disaster. Peterson recently endowed the Peter G. Peterson Foundation with a personal gift of a billion dollars, about half of his windfall from his sale of Blackstone just before the markets crashed.

As his founding president, he hired the government's former comptroller general, David Walker, a political independent with a facility for garnering good publicity with bad fiscal news. Walker in turn has functioned as a missionary for the idea that the Republic faces fiscal collapse. Many liberals think of Walker as a statesman and view his alarmism as a bulwark against Republican tax cuts. (More than $2 trillion in tax cuts later, it wasn't much of bulwark.) As an indication of his influence, here is what Jonathan Fanton, president of the moderately liberal MacArthur Foundation, recently said in a June 2008 address to the Council for Advancement and Support of Education:

> In January, I met with Comptroller General David Walker. He noted that the percentage of the U.S. population aged 65 and over will likely reach 20 percent by 2047—perhaps more, if life spans continue to increase. Spending on Medicare, Medicaid, and Social Security will more than double by 2050, from about 9 percent of GDP at present to nearly 20 percent . . . The implications for education, social services, housing programs, and more are alarming. Virtually all of MacArthur's domestic work is at risk if the federal and state governments lose their discretion to allocate needed funds to address social and economic problems.

This analysis is profoundly naive and misleading. The savaging of spending for children and social services under Reagan and both Bushes had nothing to do with Social Security and Medicare, whose problems exist in the future (and in the case of Social Security may not exist at all). And in the Clinton era, social outlay was blocked by the administration's drive for a permanent budget surplus. Under Bush II, the surplus was given away in tax cuts and war-making. It's true that entitlement programs have gradually been consuming more of the federal budget, but the cuts in other programs were caused by the hostility of right-wing presidents to social spending generally, by reckless tax cuts for the wealthy, and by increases in military spending.

"I would ask that if you leave here remembering only one number, let it be this one: $53 trillion," Peterson testified to the House Budget Committee as part of a promotional event for his foundation's launch last June. "Fifty-three trillion in today's dollars is what this country owes between our national debt, future liabilities, and our huge unfunded promises for programs like Social Security and Medicare," he continued, terming that number "unacceptable" and "un-American."

The need to reform "unfunded liabilities" has become a bipartisan mantra. However, the $53 trillion figure—others have put the figure as high as $72 trillion—is intellectually dishonest. It is derived by taking the worst-case assumptions about Medicare and Social Security, adding the national debt, assuming no change in social policy (such as universal health insurance), and extrapolating these and other projected costs into the indefinite future. As the economist Dean Baker has observed, everyone expects the Pentagon to spend hundreds of billions a year indefinitely, but we don't call this "unfunded liability" because we expect government to collect taxes to pay for it. In his 1993 book *Facing Up*, Peterson himself put the unfunded liability number at a mere $14 trillion. Any gloom-and-doom estimate that can vary by huge orders of magnitude depending on assumptions is inherently suspect.

How the Right Snookers the Center

In the spring and summer of 2008, two rival groups of influential budget experts engaged in a bitter debate about how best to constrain long-term entitlement spending. The details are a bit abstruse but well worth following, because they suggest just how disabling will be the conventional wisdom unless Obama has the nerve to transcend and demolish it.

The story begins with the radically conservative Heritage Foundation and one of its most effective strategists, Stuart Butler, an affable Briton who opposes all large-scale social outlay. Heritage has long been on a crusade to privatize both Social Security and Medicare, as well as to cut taxes and slash other social spending.

The cast of characters includes Washington's many deficit hawks—the aforementioned Pete Peterson and David Walker; the anti-deficit Concord Coalition; a bipartisan group called the Committee for a Responsible Budget; the Blue Dog caucus of fiscally conservative Democrats in Congress; and several of the more conservative people at the Brookings Institution. Brookings was once moderately liberal but has become more conservative over the years, and today it is best described as center-right, especially on budget issues.

In 2006, Stuart Butler pitched an idea to people at Brookings. What if conservatives and liberals (with liberals implausibly represented by Brookings) could unite on a bipartisan plan to solve the widely presumed catastrophe of long-term deficits in entitlement programs? The idea had both political and funding appeal. Middle-of-the-road foundations love nothing so much as bipartisanship, which reassures their trustees. And several big foundations had bought David Walker's story.

So Brookings and Heritage convened a regular working group, named the Brookings-Heritage Seminar on Fiscal Issues, whose sixteen members spanned a spectrum running from senior people from the Urban Institute in the political center, to Heritage on the far right. Four moderate-to-liberal foundations supported the splendidly bipartisan seminar, with funding of several hundred thousand dollars. This was an odd strategy for people concerned about public spending on children, housing, and other social needs. And if these foundations wanted more social outlay to materialize, about the last place on the planet to look for allies was the Heritage Foundation—a group that would not back expanded social spending no matter what the fate of Social Security and Medicare.

The seminar then set about trying to reach agreement on a set of principles. It was here that Butler and the other conservatives took the high-minded fiscal moderates to the cleaners.

Assuming, for the sake of argument, that long-term deficits were a serious problem (which is not the case), any serious fiscal bargain would include both restoration of tax revenues as well as caps on spending. In fact, Robert Rubin has spent much of the Bush era trying to promote just such a grand bargain. But in several rounds of discussion of the Brookings-Heritage Fiscal Seminar, the right-wingers around the table made it clear that taxes could not be part of the discussion; the Bush tax cuts were sacrosanct.

Anyone with an iota of worldly political wisdom or ideological conviction would have recognized that intransigence as a deal-breaker. How can social programs be on the table but not taxes? But having taken large sums from several foundations and having promised a consensus document, the group could not deadlock; it needed a "deliverable." So while the right-wingers played hard-ball, the moderates in the group just rolled over.

The ensuing alarmist joint statement was released in late March 2008 under the headline "Taking Back Our Fiscal Future." It proposed a radical remedy that had long been a goal of the Heritage Foundation—automatic caps on spending for Medicare, Medicaid, and Social Security, turning them from guaranteed programs of social insurance into ordinary outlays dependent on regular appropriations. This draconian remedy would logically lead either to privatization or to the replacement of these guaranteed programs with vouchers that would provide far less benefit.

Such an approach had been fiercely and successfully resisted by Democrats throughout the Bush era. But here were some of the most prestigious Democratic budget experts, including former senior budget officials Robert Reischauer, Alice Rivlin, and Isabel Sawhill, as well as former Clinton aide William Galston, signing on. Excluded from the supposedly broad spectrum were two of the most respected liberals on tax and budget issues, Jared Bernstein of the Economic Policy Institute and Robert Greenstein of the Center on Budget and Policy Priorities. And Brookings's own moderate liberals, economists Henry Aaron and Jason Furman, were kept in the dark about the group's very existence.

The group's composition and the report's conclusions suggest the success that the far right has in dominating public debate and in manipulating or co-opting moderates. The Heritage Foundation and the American Enterprise Institute, in other contexts, go merrily on peddling more tax cuts as the cure for all ills. But put them in a room with the Brookings Institution and the Urban Institute and they become gravely concerned about the fiscal well-being of the Republic—as long as the remedy is to destroy social insurance.

Writing on the Heritage Foundation's Web site, Butler crowed that the authors had agreed that Medicare, Medicaid, and Social Security "should be converted into regular programs that compete on a level playing field with such programs as defense, rather than pre-empting funds for these programs or automatically running up long-term deficits."

> The authors agree that certain myths are used as excuses for not tackling the entitlement problem. Among the biggest is that we can simply fix the problem by "rolling back the Bush tax cuts" and raising taxes to pay for entitlement promises. The authors agree that raising taxes to the European-style levels needed for that would "cripple the economy."

Several signers complained that they had not agreed to convert these social insurance entitlements to ordinary spending programs—only to budget caps—and the first claim was removed from the Heritage site. Aaron and Greenstein responded by organizing a rival group, which included Nobel laureate Robert Solow.

The Aaron-Greenstein expert group released its own report in early July, declaring, "We agree that the nation faces large, persistent budget deficits that would ultimately risk significant damage to the economy." But the group warned that the recommendations contained in the Brookings-Heritage report could:

> jeopardize the health and economic security of the poor, the elderly, and people with serious disabilities. For one thing, it does not focus adequate attention on the main driver of our fiscal problem—the relentless rise in health care costs throughout the U.S. health care system . . . For another, it does not propose any action to restrain the hundreds of billions of dollars in entitlements that are delivered through the tax code and flow largely to more affluent Americans.

The rival report went on to explain that "over the next 75 years, the cost just of making permanent the 2001 and 2003 tax cuts is 3½ times the size of the entire Social Security shortfall," and that tax loopholes—taken off the table in the Brookings-Heritage report—consume $900 billion a year.

As Greenstein points out, the most politically damaging thing about the Brookings-Heritage document is that it uses moderate Democrats—the senior budget experts whom a President Obama would be likely to consult—to validate the far-right storyline: that the nation's fiscal problems have everything to do with social insurance and nothing to do with tax cuts or the failure to achieve comprehensive health reform.

Why did the likes of Reischauer, Sawhill, and Rivlin let themselves be used in this fashion? After three or more decades on the front lines of budget wars, each seems to have given up on more imaginative possibilities and become a crusader for limiting entitlements.

For Sawhill, the conflict is generational. The old, she believes, get relatively too much via Social Security and Medicare, and the corollary is that the young get too little. As she writes in a recent article for Brookings:

> Right now, thanks to the current contract, older Americans are the only group in our society that has access to universal, fee-for-service medical care. Younger Americans do not have such access, have seen their incomes stagnate in recent years, and yet will be expected to pay for the current generation's morally indefensible fiscal policies. As a result, without a major change, working-age families and their children will not receive the kind of help that will eventually make the nation more productive. And a country that gives priority to its elderly over its young is arguably a country that doesn't have much of a future. A new contract, then, would tighten the flow of funds to older generations and invest more resources in younger families and their children.

But why not expand the social contract to the young rather than withdraw it from the old? Why not pay for universal pre-kindergarten by repealing the Bush tax cuts rather than by gutting Social Security benefits? This is the kind of weary, stunted liberal imagination that Obama will have to challenge.

Reischauer, now president of the Urban Institute, told me that he felt it was necessary for a high-profile, ideologically diverse group to propose a drastic remedy. In testimony before the Senate Budget Committee last year, Reischauer downplayed the impact of tax cuts. Federal revenues, he noted, were "about at their postwar average." He added: "Clearly, we must look elsewhere for the roots of the severe future budget imbalance predicted for the future. And those roots are to be found in the retirement-related entitlement programs—Social Security, Medicare, and Medicaid."

Reischauer has even been wary of expanded health insurance coverage, lest increased access produce additional costs. "Does the total system need to be reformed? Yes, but it's unlikely to be done in a way that will save costs. The interest groups are too powerful," he told me. Speaking of the dueling budget statements, Reischauer added, "I was furious when I saw how Stuart characterized this on his Web site, and I would not be surprised if this how he characterizes our statement in his speeches."

Then why get in bed with the likes of Stuart Butler? "Congress is going have to grapple with this, and there are people like Stuart in Congress," Reischauer said. "We need to figure out where there is common ground." But as orchestrated by Butler and Heritage, the common ground has been defined as people with basically kindred views, like Greenstein and Reischauer, being in warring camps—while those whose social philosophies are worlds apart, like Reischauer and Butler, are in the same club.

On "entitlements," the fiscal moderates have bought the idea of emphasizing cuts in spending first. On Medicare, they've accepted the right's premise that the idea that true national health insurance is politically inconceivable, even though it would produce great cost savings by eliminating expensive middlemen. And since national health insurance is out of the question, we might as well hack away at Medicare and Medicaid.

But as the Greenstein-Aaron report points out, capping Medicare and Medicaid would not solve the general problem of inflation in health costs. It would only "threaten the central achievement of those programs—providing the elderly, the disabled, and the poor with access to the same kind of health care that other Americans receive."

So here is what Obama faces in terms of conventional budgetary wisdom. On the center right, some of Washington's most prestigious Democratic budget experts are willing to put Social Security, Medicare, and Medicaid on the chopping block before addressing the issue of Bush's multitrillion-dollar tax cut. On the center left, good liberals such as Greenstein and Aaron are also alarmed about long-term deficits in entitlement programs but want tax increases to be part of the deal.

Aaron is brave enough to say we can't do Medicare reform without general health insurance reform. Greenstein, to his great credit, says he believes that increased deficits are needed in a severe recession, and that Social Security and Medicare as entitlement programs can be saved with sensible reforms—but it is a mark of how far to the right the consensus has swung that Aaron and Greenstein are on the left edge of this conversation.

It will take true leadership from the White House to explain that no, Social Security is not in crisis; that the hysteria about "entitlements" is right-wing ideology masquerading as fiscal high-mindedness; that the cure for Medicare's problems is universal health insurance; that the cupboard is in fact not bare if we revise taxing and spending priorities. A President Obama would also need to refrain from taking his budget advice from these conservative onetime liberals, who are still generally considered the cream of Democratic fiscal experts. And he would need to explain to the American people why austerity is in fact not the right cure for recession.

2. Government is perverse or incompetent.

Who said the following?

> Government cannot solve our problems, it can't set our goals, it cannot define our vision. Government cannot eliminate poverty or provide a bountiful economy or reduce inflation or save our cities or cure illiteracy or provide energy. And government cannot mandate goodness.

Ronald Reagan? No, those were the words of President Jimmy Carter, in his 1978 State of the Union address. And who said this?

> We know big government does not have all the answers. We know there's not a program for every problem. We

have worked to give the American people a smaller, less bureaucratic government in Washington. And we have to give the American people one that lives within its means.

The era of big government is over.

George W. Bush? Actually, that was Bill Clinton, in his State of the Union address, in January 1996. Clinton added with pride, "Today our federal government is 200,000 employees smaller than it was the day I took office as President."

The irony is that the rest of Clinton's speech went on to propose a long list of widely shared goals that only government could achieve—clean up the environment, improve job security, restore educational opportunity. His conceit was that he could combine smaller government and even disparagement of government with a commitment to more nimble government. But his headline message undermined the details of his program and his ability to win support for it. He pandered to what he took to be the fashion of the day, and triangulated himself into a corner of his own making.

Just for the record, here is the original rather than the imitation, from Ronald Reagan's first inaugural address:

In this present crisis, government is not the solution to our problem; government is the problem.

Except among resolutely progressive Democrats, it has become de rigueur to disparage government and praise markets, or to include disclaimers about the limits of government.

This has been the particular mantra of "third-way" organizations such as the Democratic Leadership Council. It has infected (and undercut) recent Democratic presidential nominees. Democrats mistakenly view such rhetoric as bulletproofing them against right-wing caricatures of liberals—but all it does is to reinforce Republican ideology. This kind of rhetoric makes the fatal mistake of playing on the other side's turf.

As the linguist and close student of political rhetoric Geoffrey Nunberg has written,

> The Democrats' big mistake has been to imagine that they could neutralize the big-government issue simply by adopting the Republicans' rhetoric and disparaging traditional liberalism in the bargain. Writing in 2000, White House speechwriter Michael Waldman noted that within a few years after Clinton had announced the end of big government, "the tax-cutting, government-hating strain of the GOP had lost its political potency." That proved to be less than prophetic. Notwithstanding Clinton's considerable accomplishments in reducing the actual size of government, those on the right scarcely missed a beat: They interpreted Clinton's pronounce-ment as a concession speech, an admission of the bankruptcy of the policies that conservatives had been attacking since the days of the New Deal. *The Weekly Standard* made that crystal clear in the headline it gave to its story on Clinton's speech: "We Win!" And rhetori-cally speaking, they were dead right.

Redeeming Government

As we saw in chapter 2, the most effective Democratic presidents did not shrink from their embrace of government to achieve national purposes and to help ordinary people.

In his celebrated keynote address to the Democratic National Convention in August 2004, the speech that established him as a potential president even before he had won election to the US Senate, Obama demonstrated how to talk about national unity in a manner that deftly moved the ideological debate onto the Democrats' home court, paving the way for more activist use of government:

Alongside our famous individualism, there's another
ingredient in the American saga: A belief that we're all
connected as one people. If there is a child on the south
side of Chicago who can't read, that matters to me, even
if it's not my child. If there's a senior citizen somewhere
who can't pay for their prescription drugs, and has to
choose between medicine and the rent, that makes my
life poorer, even if it's not my grandparent. If there's an
Arab American family being rounded up without benefit
of an attorney or due process, that threatens my civil
liberties.

This eloquent and personal passage did not mention government per se—but what other institution is going to underwrite
good schools and affordable medical care? And which party is
more likely to manage government in a way that doesn't arbi-
trarily diminish rights? This brand of leadership links the
national desire for unity and common purpose with a redemption of a progressive Democratic party as custodian of a social
compact. The real issues are *who leads* government, and what we
need government to achieve.

The think tank Demos, where I have the honor to be a senior
fellow, operates a program called Public Works, which addresses
how political leaders can bring about, and talk about, effective
government. The essence of the work is the idea that government is a set of public structures that we as citizens create and
rely on to help people and businesses. Government helps us
protect ourselves from risks we cannot face alone. Government is
both the product and locus of political democracy—and only as
good as our democracy. Our democratic institutions are where we
come together to plan for the common good; they are the steward
of our environment and future. If these structures are dismantled,
disparaged, chronically underfunded, or eroded from within, all
citizens are the poorer.

In keeping with its mission, Demos also trains leaders to

talk effectively about government. It is a little sad that many progressives need to relearn the art of talking up government. To the best politicians, it comes naturally. But as the free market demonstrates its genius for financial catastrophe, at least some Democratic leaders are speaking in a stronger voice.

For example, Deval Patrick, the first Democrat to be elected governor of Massachusetts in sixteen years, began his inaugural address in January 2007 with these words:

> For a very long time now we have been told that government is bad, that it exists only to serve the powerful and well-connected, that its job is not important enough to be done by anyone competent, let alone committed, and that all of us are on our own. Today we join together in common cause to lay that fallacy to rest, and to extend a great movement based on shared responsibility from the corner office to the corner of your block and back again.

At almost the same moment, Colorado governor Bill Ritter, a progressive Democrat in a swing state, said at his inauguration:

> Let's fulfill the Colorado Promise by ending the crisis of the uninsured and enacting comprehensive health-care reform. Let's fulfill the Colorado Promise by creating good jobs and fixing our transportation system. And by being stubborn stewards of our land, our air, our water and our wildlife.
>
> Let's fulfill the Colorado Promise by living up to our part of the social compact. Such an important part of who we are as a state, and really as a nation, is the social compact—the covenant that says government exists for the people, for all people. It exists to provide legitimate public functions. It exists to ensure we take care of seniors, and the disabled, and for those who struggle mightily—

whatever the reason. Government has a responsibility to intersect with their struggle, looking always for ways to improve the quality of their lives.

Pennsylvania governor Ed Rendell was even more explicit about the need for expansive government in a recent speech calling for a transformed national energy policy. Recounting the several creative steps his state had taken to promote renewable energy, Rendell asked for bolder leadership from Washington:

> Throughout American history, our biggest challenges have been met by just that type of federal leadership. President Roosevelt took charge and provided the resources to create the Manhattan Project and the National Institutes of Health. President Kennedy did the same to take us to the Moon. The atom bomb, the virtual eradication of polio, the Apollo launch—these challenges were surmounted because our federal government united the great minds, found the funds, and put in place the policies necessary to ensure success.

My colleague Miles Rapoport, before becoming president of Demos, served fourteen years as an elected state government official in Connecticut. He did not flinch from advocating taxes adequate to support high-quality state services. In arguing for enactment of a state income tax, he said:

> Low taxes is not an economic strategy; it is simply a race to a bottom we can never reach. Excellent education, a transportation system that works effectively, investment in research, a vibrant arts culture, and a clean environment are the ways our state can stand out. And paying for those things is a price we can't afford not to pay.

There are several good books on the great things government

has done and can do. If Obama has not yet read them, he owes it to himself and to America to do so. A fine example is political scientist Paul Light's 2002 book *Government's Greatest Achievements*, which includes a top-fifty list of Government's Greatest Endeavors. They run the gamut from ensuring safe food and drinking water to increasing access to education to promoting scientific and technical research. Two items on Light's list have a bittersweet taste given recent events: Increasing the Stability of Financial Markets and Expanding Homeownership—illustrating what happens when conservatives promiscuously undermine government. If we are lucky, his 2012 edition will include: Rescuing America from the Great Financial Collapse of 2007–09.

Among the too-rare efforts to credit what government does well is the program on Innovations in American Government, initiated more than twenty years ago through a partnership of Harvard's Kennedy School of Government and the Ford Foundation. Since 1986, the program has sought out and evaluated over 300 of the most promising innovations in American government each year and given awards to the best. For example, it gave early recognition to ComStat, the New York City police administration and data-tracking system that reduced crime, which has been adapted by city and state governments across the country. The Innovations program has recognized cutting-edge innovative federal improvements at the much-maligned Department of Veterans Affairs, and called attention to environmental protection measures in western states that rely not on top-down regulation but on cooperative agreements with stakeholders in watershed or forest environments.

The point is not that government always succeeds. Like other complex enterprises, such as large corporations, it has its failures as well as its successes. But in the current environment the media, reinforced by politicians of both parties, report almost exclusively about government failures, while downplaying the successes.

On the wall of my study is a poster created by the Council for Excellence in Government. It reads in part:

They created the internet.

Set the standard for auto safety.

Cleaned up our water.

And now they're working to ensure every child is
immunized.

Where can you buy shares in a company like this?

You can't.

Because it's already yours. It's your federal, state,
and local government.

If it were a company, it would be hailed for
innovation and change. But because it's our
government, it doesn't always get the credit it
deserves.

We need more leaders to start talking this way, starting with our
president.

3. Tax relief is the best benefit that government can deliver.

Since Reagan, the Republicans have played a well-established
game of cutting taxes, mostly on the rich, then bemoaning the
resulting deficits and cutting social outlay. The Democrats then
come back in and, playing the role of fiscal stewards, raise taxes
and further trim social spending, thus denying themselves the
asset that made them the majority party for much of the middle
third of the twentieth century—the ability to use government to
help ordinary people.

By branding Democrats as the party of "tax-and-spend" while
denying them the money to do more than token spending,
Republicans put Democrats into a fiscal box. But the box is partly
of the Democrats' own making. Many Democrats have been
persuaded that raising taxes is unpopular, but politically possible if
they do two things: First, raise taxes only on the rich; and second,
make sure to also cut taxes on the middle and working class.

This defensive strategy sounds good, but it has two fatal flaws. For one, it reinforces the general anti-tax mood. For another, it denies the government the revenues necessary to transform an economy marked by increasing instability, inequality, and insecurity. Give away substantial revenue in the form of tax credits and there is nothing left for major program initiatives. In the eras of FDR and LBJ, tax credits were a very small part of the total progressive arsenal. But if you look at recent Democratic social policy initiatives, most of them are packaged as tax credits.

Sometimes, tax credits make sense, as in the case of the Earned Income Tax Credit for low- and moderate-income breadwinners. The EITC is "refundable": If you qualify for the EITC, the government sends you a check, even if you owe no taxes. It is a wage subsidy by another name; and it's a reflection of our political era that Congress would never enact a direct wage subsidy, but loves the EITC, which gives politicians bragging rights about tax cutting.

Many Democrats have accepted tax credits as policies to serve social goals—the best half-a-loaf they can get during an era of anti-government and anti-tax sentiment. But going with the flow just reinforces that sentiment.

Tax credits are often bad policy. They blow huge holes in the tax code. Unlike direct subsidies, tax credits are automatically available to any class of taxpayer who qualifies, so they are poorly targeted. They tend to distort economic decision making on the part of taxpayers, and they deny government the ability to be selective. They turn the IRS into a social policy agency, a job for which it is ill suited. Even the widely praised EITC is a second-best substitute for a comprehensive labor-market and income policy.

With the exception of refundable credits such as the EITC, tax preferences also tend to be regressive. For instance, the sacrosanct homeowners' deduction for interest and local property taxes is worth far more to a rich homeowner than a poor one. The tax credits on low-income rental housing come in the form of tax breaks for developers and for investors who buy a share of the artificial tax losses. A lot of the tax subsidy that presumably is intended by Congress to subsidize affordable rental housing ends up in the pockets of rich middlemen.

A direct subsidy would be a much more efficient way to produce more affordable housing. But a tax break has become the course of least resistance because it ostensibly doesn't increase public spending. This is a total fiction, since a dollar of forgone revenues is equal to a dollar of program outlay.

Moreover, while there has been justified criticism of "earmarks"— the process of adding special provisions into appropriations bills to favor one constituent or a very narrow group—the process of creating tax credits suffers from exactly the same problems. Critics of earmarks point out that they are hardly ever subjected to normal legislative hearings; rather, deals are cut behind closed doors and the general public only learns the true intended beneficiary afterward, if ever. By the same token, the tax-writing committees are far from transparent. Narrow tax benefits are often added to bills without hearings. And unlike appropriations, which have to be reviewed and scrutinized annually, tax loopholes are stuck in the tax code indefinitely. For a politician, it is much more pleasurable to bestow a tax credit than to close a loophole.

George W. Bush and John McCain have both proposed to address the crisis of health insurance with new programs of tax credits. This approach does nothing to reform the structural flaws in the current health insurance system—it merely subsidizes demand; and the credit is invariably proposed at too low a level to allow the beneficiary to afford decent health insurance.

So when they propose mainly tax credits, Democrats increasingly play on Republican turf and reinforce Republican ideology: Government bad, tax cuts good. The game becomes a battle merely over which taxes to cut. Look at recent Democratic proposals to address social ills from self-described New Democrats, and you will see primarily tax credits. Consider, for example, an extensive policy paper titled "Playing Offense on Taxes," published by the group Third Way, in February.

The group proposes a long list of tax cuts and tax credits to be embraced by Democrats: doubling the tax credit for child care; adding a "new baby" credit; a tax credit for half the cost of college tuition; a tax credit for first-time home buyers; a special onetime tax credit for homeowners caught in the subprime squeeze; a tax credit for the cost of caring for aging parents; a permanent increase in the corporate tax credit for research and development; business tax credits for investing in broadband infrastructure; a permanent increase in tax breaks for new business investment; and other credits for small business. Total cost in lost revenue: $345 billion over ten years.

Except for the fact that the entire set of initiatives is run through the tax code, it sounds almost like a parody of fairly typical Democrat government spending programs—so much for a "third way." But by using tax breaks, the strategy ignores the need for structural reforms and careful targeting. Maybe what America needs is not tax credits for child care, but funding for a high-quality child-care *system*. Rather than relying so heavily on tax subsidies to corporations, we need to revamp our public programs of research and development, and design a national strategy for increasing our broadband capacity. And isn't it time to revisit the way we finance higher education? Relying entirely on tax credits reinforces existing systems, and the idea that all of this is the individual's problem.

In a nightmare movie parody suggested by my friend and colleague Michael Lipsky, titled *The Last Tax Break,* Congress, in a frenzy of Republican enthusiasm, goes on a tax-loophole rampage and for good measure cuts taxes for everyone across the board. In the morning government has disappeared entirely.

Barack Obama's campaign has mostly avoided this pattern. Blueprint for Change, the campaign's basic platform document, described as Obama's Plan for America, offers dozens of policy proposals, including just a few tax breaks. Some of these are good policy. For instance, he proposes to cut the income tax by $1,000 for working families to partly offset the regressive payroll taxes they pay. Likewise his proposed credit for homeowners who do not itemize deductions and are thus denied the benefit of the mortgage interest write-off.

He would also eliminate all income taxes on seniors earning less than $50,000 a year. But statistically, seniors (thanks to Social Security and Medicare) are no worse off than working-aged Americans, and it's not clear why they deserve special tax favoritism. This seems less a sensible policy than a calculated pitch for the senior vote. The structural problem for seniors, moreover, is an inadequate and worsening pension system, and Obama's proposals on that front are fairly meager.

Obama proposes to expand the child-care tax credit, though he would also dramatically expand the system of child care and pre-kindergarten. He also proposes a refundable $4,000 tax credit—equivalent to a direct grant—for community college tuition. It would also be available to other college students who completed a hundred hours a year of volunteer service.

Unfortunately, one of Obama's latest initiatives is a proposed tax credit to help small businesses purchase health insurance for employees. One can understand the allure of this idea during a campaign when Obama needs to reassure business elites that he is not a Bolshevik. But these moves also reinforce right-wing ideology, add loopholes to the tax system, and distract us from needed systemic reforms.

The next president ought to spend some political capital to educate Americans on good tax policy and bad. On balance, Obama's reliance on tax breaks is less excessive than that of many Democrats (and virtually all Republicans), but his embrace of some dubious tax schemes suggests the seductiveness of the approach, even to progressives. This argument dates back at least to President Kennedy. When faced with a need to stimulate the economy in a recession, the Kennedy administration was divided, with chief economist Walter Heller recommending tax cuts and adviser-at-large John Kenneth Galbraith calling for public spending to repair public systems that had deteriorated in the Eisenhower years. Taking the course of least resistance and the one favored by business lobbies, Kennedy sided with Heller and sent Galbraith off to be ambassador to India. Ever since then, conservatives proposing tax cuts as a recovery measure have pointed to liberal John Kennedy as a role model.

4. The private sector is invariably more efficient than the public.

The first recent president to embrace this view was not Ronald Reagan, but Jimmy Carter, who sent Congress legislation deregulating industry after industry. Carter's conservatism on this issue was reinforced by the work of right-wing think tanks such as the Heritage Foundation, the American Enterprise Institute, and the Cato Institute. As Republican ideology became dominant in the 1980s and 1990s, many Democrats sought to emulate the Republicans by insisting that they, too, appreciated markets.

For center-right Democrats, embracing the free-market view offered two short-term political benefits. First, it associated Democrats with an ideology supposedly in fashion. Second, it paid huge dividends in campaign contributions from organized businesses. The Democrat who wants to regulate business is as popular on Wall Street as the picnic skunk. The one who embraces Republican-style deregulation and privatization is praised as a sound thinker and rewarded with donations. The influence of big money in pushing Democrats to the right is part of the undertow, and worth a whole book of its own.

Relearning the Virtues and Limits of Markets

Markets are competent much of the time to do many things. In normal everyday commerce, the discipline of supply and demand efficiently signals producers of the preferences of consumers and produces roughly appropriate prices. However, there are many things society needs that are not efficiently produced at the right price and quantity by market forces.

Markets are unreliable in four key respects. They price many critical goods and services wrong, among them health, education, research, pollution costs, and complex financial instruments. They produce a socially indefensible income distribution. Left to their own devices, they produce periodic euphorias, panics, and depressions. And they have an unfortunate tendency to put on the auction block things that should be beyond price, such as political democracy and human life itself. We see this as public parks, schools, spaces, and the public spirit give way to literal or figurative gated communities without concern for the cost to the democratic commons. Adam Smith, who was most famous for his claim that acts of individual selfishness aggregated to general economic efficiency based on the discipline of supply and demand, also wrote: "How selfish soever man may be supposed, there are evidently some principles in his nature, which interest him in the fortune of others, and render their happiness necessary to him . . ."

Absent government investment and regulation, markets create grotesque income inequalities. The market is geared to satisfy consumer demands at any given distribution of income and wealth. The market is agnostic about income disparities and their civic consequences. Without government help, less affluent people could not afford either education for their children or basic medical care—and education and health consume about 25 percent of GDP right off the bat. A society divided into billionaires and paupers also reinforces the political power of economic elites to lobby for even weaker government counterweights. Grotesque extremes of income and wealth are reflected—and reinforced—in disparities of political influence.

Economists refer to positive or negative "externalities," meaning costs or benefits to society that are not fully captured in the price of a given transaction, but rather are "externalized" onto society. Pollution is a negative externality. The cost to a polluting industry of dumping waste into a stream is far less than the true cost to society. In the crisis of global climate change, markets priced the true costs of carbon emissions incompletely; and markets in the absence of government intervention had no way of compensating for their own myopia.

Research, by contrast, is a positive externality. The benefit of a medical breakthrough that can be captured by a university researcher or a particular company is less than the broad benefit to society. Since basic research is also something of a gamble, the private market as a whole tends to underinvest in research.

And despite the artificial construct of markets-versus-governments, markets are always structured by rules that include everything from bankruptcy and patent mechanisms to the terms of property ownership itself. The broad point is that markets deliver better for most people when government counterweights complement what markets can't do, and constrain what markets do recklessly.*

Many Democrats, however, are still in the habit of using the word *marketlike* as a verbal amulet to ward off the curse of being charged with the sin of favoring government. To speak fondly of markets is to invite campaign contributions from the affluent. To speak of markets is feel modern; to rely on government is to seem mired in the 1930s. But after the experience of recent years, when financial markets are again mired in 1930s-style collapse, it's time to revisit old verities. To invert Ronald Reagan, the market is often the problem, not the solution.

After the subprime collapse, I accepted an invitation to testify before Congress from a progressive Democrat whom I much admire, Representative Barney Frank, who chairs the House

---

*For a full treatment of this story, the reader is invited to consult my 1997 book *Everything for Sale: The Virtues and Limits of Markets* and the sequel published in 2007, *The Squandering of America*, recounting the gradual dismantling of financial regulation and warning of an economic crash. An earlier book of mine, *The Economic Illusion: False Choices Between Prosperity and Social Justice* (1984), explains how good public policy can optimize both equality and efficiency.

Committee on Financial Services. Chairman Frank was trying to rally his committee and the Congress to the idea that a new generation of financial regulations was required to prevent repetition of a new generation of abuses. That was in October 2007, when the scale of the collapse was still unfolding.

At that stage of the crisis, however, even Barney Frank took pains to point out that free markets were great innovators and that we needed to take care not to discourage innovations. This disclaimer was politically necessary for a liberal chairman fighting an uphill battle against the conventional wisdom that markets could do few wrongs. Despite my esteem for Representative Frank and my appreciation for the invitation, I begged to differ. Some innovations, I testified, are far worse than no innovation. The country would have been far better off if financial engineers had not invented some of the toxic mortgage products that went on to poison financial markets. It was government's job to keep these harmful "innovations" from the public. Frank, of course, agreed in substance. But it was instructive to see how carefully he couched his call for reform in the idiom of respect for markets.

Since then, Frank has grown even bolder and has exerted real ideological as well as policy leadership. "We are in a worldwide crisis now because of excessive deregulation," Frank told *Washington Post* columnist E. J. Dionne in July. With the 1999 repeal of the Glass-Steagall Act, Frank added, "We let investment banks get into a much wider range of activities without regulation," seeding the subprime mortgage mess and the cascading calamity in banking.

Even after the subprime collapse, however, some Democrats find it difficult to articulate a full-throated defense of the necessary role of government investment and regulation, which is of course the flip side of market failure. This reticence is the consequence of three decades of relentless propagandizing to the effect that markets are always better; it reflects continuing Democratic solicitude of Wall Street. It will take exceptional presidential leadership and the use of the presidency as teacher to explain to the public what markets do well and where they fail. Obama clearly has the skills to do that. We shall soon see whether he has the nerve.

5. Successful Democrats talk more like Republicans.

Until very recently, too many Democratic political experts— pollsters, strategists, admen, and campaign consultants—have tended to reinforce their candidates' impulses to be feeble rather than bold advocates of the use of government to constrain market excesses and to help ordinary Americans. The dynamics of this disease operate in multiple and reinforcing ways.

In the fall of 2007, an advocacy organization called the Herndon Group was promoting a particular brand of health-care reform, which they called Quality Affordable Choice. They were aided by the respected Democratic polling firm Lake Research Partners. Specifically, they were trying to demonstrate the appeal of a version not unlike Bill Clinton's, as updated by the political scientist Jacob Hacker.

Under the proposal, Americans could choose among any of several high-quality plans offered by the private insurance industry, with the stipulation that discrimination against people with preexisting conditions would be prohibited. Consumers could keep their existing coverage if they chose, or select another private plan, or a public one. Hacker himself offers a more robust version than Herndon did, freely acknowledging that he has devised his plan as the most politically realistic stepping-stone to national health insurance. I like Hacker's strategy, but I was appalled at how the Herndon Group tried to market it.

In its analysis, widely presented to liberal groups, Herndon sought to demonstrate that Republican-style "health savings accounts" or tax credits on the right and Medicare-for-all plans on the left had less voter appeal than their own preferred approach. However, they put a subtle thumb on the scale in the way they worded the descriptions of the various approaches that were read to focus groups.

Their own preferred plan was described as "An approach that would guarantee affordable health insurance coverage for every American with a choice of private or public plans that cover all necessary medical services, paid for by employers and individuals on a sliding scale." Medicare-for-all was described as "A single government-financed health insurance plan for all Americans financed by tax dollars that would pay private health care providers for a comprehensive set of medical services." Obviously, a genuine defender of Medicare-for-all could have composed far more attractive language without sacrificing accuracy.

The nuances of language are worth savoring. Herndon's version of their preferred plan hit all the notes that registered positively—"choice," "guaranteed," "affordable," "all necessary medical services." Oddly, even though Medicare is the one system that guarantees total choice of doctors and hospitals, their description of Medicare-for-all was not adorned with any of the positive attributes that they reserved for their own plan. Rather, their characterization of Medicare used terms that pollsters knew would trigger ambivalence—"single," "government-financed," "tax dollars." Not surprisingly, given the stacked deck, the Herndon representatives reported that their own plan polled best.

In making their case, the Herndon representatives did one other curious thing. In pooh-poohing the rival Medicare-for-all approach, they cited supposed findings from their focus groups that Medicare wasn't as popular as it once was: "Voters strongly support Medicare but believe it has problems. Because of those problems, people are wary of using it as a model." (And just to be sure, Herndon's own language reinforced this skepticism.) Yes, this ambivalence may have been the fault of Republicans for underfunding Medicare and partly privatizing it, but these days many citizens experience the same frustrations with Medicare as with private insurance plans. Herndon's presenters warned Democrats not to become too closely aligned with Medicare.

But hold on. Medicare, after all, is one of the Democrats' crown jewels. Poll after poll has shown that even with Bush's mischief, seniors still value it immensely. Medicare is Democrats' core philosophy made flesh—namely: There are some things the private sector can't and won't do, like providing reliable health insurance for the elderly. Comprehensive social programs often are not just more equitable *but more cost-effective* than layers of private-sector middlemen being bribed, expensively and half-heartedly, to meet social goals. If Republicans are weakening Medicare and partly privatizing it (as Bush had shrewdly done), isn't the remedy to fight back and associate Democrats with the robust brand of Medicare that citizens so clearly value?

As it got criticisms from some groups that heard its presentation, Herndon pulled back slightly from its advice that Democrats should not get too cozy with Medicare. But fast-forward a year.

It is July 2008, and Democrats, urged on by a bedridden Senator Ted Kennedy, recovering from surgery and chemotherapy for brain cancer, have belatedly decided to wage a real fight over Medicare. Specifically, they are pushing legislation to halt the Bush scheme to expand privatization of Medicare and pay for the increased middlemen costs by cutting payments to doctors. What better demonstration of how privatization harms doctors, patients, and taxpayers alike? What better squeeze play on Republicans?

Senate Democrats will be close to the two-thirds majority they need to overturn Bush's threatened veto of the bill, but are one vote short of the senators they need to break a filibuster. And then, in an eerie echo of Clair Engle's decisive 1964 vote on civil rights, Ted Kennedy, warned by his doctors that his immune system is still fragile from the chemotherapy and to avoid crowds, bursts into the Senate chamber to cast the decisive vote. Cheers erupt. Kennedy is mobbed and hugged. The Democrats' bill passes both houses by veto-proof margins—because Republicans don't want to be perceived as voting to weaken Medicare. Apparently, there is some value for Democrats to associate themselves with Medicare after all.

Playing to Weakness

Here's how some Democratic use of polling and focus groups rein-forces equivocation. The pollster will listen to voter concerns in focus groups, then construct "test messages" and see which of them most appeals to the focus group and most inclines them to vote for the Democrat. The winning message is used to influence the candidate's actual message.

By asking questions within the existing frame, however, the pollster frequently ends up reinforcing that frame and discour-aging the impulses of intuitive political leaders to change the frame. What works in the laboratory often backfires in real poli-tics. Often the finding is that the more carefully qualified message tests better. But in real life, that tends to constrain the candidate's own gut instincts, which are often better than the consultant's. And it sends a meta-message more powerful than the ostensible, carefully qualified message about the issue: *This guy doesn't seem to know what he stands for.*

Messages composed for focus groups often sound like they were written by someone who never ran for office. The messages rarely sound like the way real people talk. It doesn't help that the most influential Democratic pollsters and consultants all have seven-figure incomes and corporate clients on the side. At best, this subtly influences their own ideological predispositions, and often it creates explicit conflicts of interest that harm their Democratic clients. Mark Penn, the strategic guru who provided what turned out to be disastrous advice for his client Hillary Clinton, is also CEO of Burson-Marsteller, a firm with many big-business clients, including the badly tarnished mercenary contractor Blackwater and one of the worst subprime offenders, Countrywide. In early 2008, at a crucial stage of the nomination battle, when Hillary Clinton was distancing herself from trade deals such as NAFTA and its progeny, the Colombia FTA, Penn was on retainer to the government of Colombia for a total of $300,000 to market the deal in the United States.

In the era now mercifully coming to a close, the Democrats' problem was not a few bad pollsters. It was systemic. Late in 2005, a mutual friend asked me if I would read a manuscript in progress by a behavioral psychologist and amateur political analyst whom I had never heard of. His name was Drew Westen, a professor at Emory University. The manuscript, titled *The Political Brain*, was the best thing I had read in many years on why Democrats lose winnable elections.

Westen's book must be read in its entirely to appreciate its subtlety and brilliance, but here is the essence of the argument. People think with an emotional brain as well as a rational brain. Republicans as a party have figured out how to engage the emotional brain, and a great many Democrats haven't. Others, such as George Lakoff, had made similar arguments, but Westen got deeper into the pathologies in the practice of politics.

As Westen noted, Al Gore lost the 2000 election in part because he came across as a robotic candidate. After the election, Gore began speaking out on the environment with a wit and a passion that electrified audiences. Where was that Al Gore when we needed him? It turned out that Gore's "expert" campaign consultants, based on a static reading of polls, had advised him to avoid talking about the environment because it wasn't a first-tier issue that moved voters. What they totally missed was that it moved *Gore* and allowed him to demonstrate his own passion, warmth, and leadership. By depriving him of his most effective passion, they weakened him as a candidate.

Westen made a second key point. Most Democrats were surprisingly squeamish about being tough—in two senses. Westen meant both tough on issues, and tough when personally attacked. As a result, voters drew two fatal conclusions: Democrats didn't quite know what they stood for. And if their stances seemed weak and equivocal in general, then they probably weren't tough enough either to defend the nation or to fight for the needs of ordinary voters.

Democratic campaign experts tended to reinforce yet another

disastrous habit. If polls show that a majority of the voters have certain predispositions, campaign consultants urged the candidate to play to those prejudices. The result is speeches in which Democratic candidates make an argument, then take part of it back with a disclaimer. Viewed statically, this kind of talk hits all the bases of public opinion as divined by polling, so it must be right. But viewed dynamically, it signals that the candidate stands for mush.

This bad advice caused many Democratic to lose winnable elections. Even worse, when Democrats did get elected, the same habits of equivocation (and the same consultants) followed them into office.

As we have seen from the examples of Lincoln, Roosevelt, LBJ, and Reagan, leadership often entails staking out a position *not* held by a majority of voters, and bringing the people around. The leadership can be good or bad, based in reality or delusion and deception (and one must hope that the truth will ultimately prove whether the leadership was worthy). But it is never simply a case of seeing where the country is, and going there. The epigraph of this chapter—"There go my people, I must find out where they are going so I can lead them"—is usually quoted in ridicule, but in Democratic politics consultants have earned huge fees by offering it as strategic advice.

In early 2005, as Democrats were mourning yet another needless election loss, *Washington Monthly* writer Amy Sullivan published one of the most widely circulated articles of the season, titled "Fire the Consultants." Democrats, she pointed out, kept hiring the same cabal of consultants whose bad advice kept losing elections. Bob Shrum, who had a perfect record of seven losses in seven presidential races, was considered a genius. Her witty article offered three reasons for this paradox. First, many consultants who were good at tactical field operations—whipping campaign machinery into shape—ended up offering strategic guidance, at which they were often incompetent. Second, there were flagrant conflicts of interest. In their career paths, consultants would win a race or two, then work their way into the Democratic Party's institutional machinery such as the Democratic Senate Campaign Committee. If a candidate then wanted the DSCC's support, he or she hired one of its operatives, all of whom ran businesses on the side. Mark Mellman, the DSCC's chief pollster in the disastrous 2002 midterm election when Democrats lost control of the Senate, went on to become John Kerry's pollster. He was a key source of the advice that Kerry should refrain from attacking Bush. Incompetent consultants have a career path of falling upward.

Third, Sullivan added, "The consultants are filling a vacuum. After all, someone has to formulate the message that a candidate can use to win the voters' support. Conservatives have spent 30 years and billions of dollars on think tanks and other organizations to develop a set of interlinked policies and language that individual Republican candidates and campaigns can adopt in plug-and-play fashion. Liberals are far behind in this message development game."

Westen, Sullivan, and Lakoff offer superb critiques. Yet each in his or her own way leaves out the one crucial element that links all these peculiar lapses. The Democrats, after all, spend almost as much money as a party as the Republicans do. They include a lot of intelligent people. So how can it be that Republicans are systematically smarter about understanding how voters' brains work (Lakoff) or stupider about continuing to hire losing consultants (Sullivan) or suffer a collective tin ear when it comes to political language (Westen)?

The missing link in the explanation is this. Republicans have been clear and unequivocal in having a core set of principles, and in taking political risks to advance it. They may occasionally lose support on some of the particulars, but they win points for their resolve. Once, that was a good description of Democrats—in the era of Roosevelt, Truman, Kennedy, and Johnson. But between 1976 and 2006, Democratic presidential candidates tended to run from their party's core beliefs. No wonder they sounded like mush. The Democrats' collective tin ear was no accident. Where Republican campaign professionals were movement conservatives and tended to sharpen Republicans' resolve, many Democratic pollsters tended to reinforce Democrats' tendency to equivocate. And it is literally impossible to deliver a forceful message filled with equivocation.

Putting aside the details of policy issues, consider the meta-message of the past twenty-eight years: Republicans may run roughshod occasionally, but they keep the country safe. I don't like a lot of [Reagan's, Bush's] positions, but at least you know where he stands.

Even someone as verbally incoherent as George W. Bush could be made to sound like a leader because he was anchored in a coherent set of principles. Free market good, government bad. Poor people are the consequence of poor values. America must be strong. Even Bush could remember that much. In the end, however, no amount of technique or resolution could compensate for policies that drove the economy aground.

Recovering Democratic Voice

Since 2006, these trends have been changing for the better. In a July 2007 analytical piece for the group Democracy Corps, James Carville and Stanley Greenberg, two Democratic campaign consultants who don't counsel equivocation, reported on their test of two different ad messages in a swing Congressional district in Illinois.

> The first . . . takes a positive approach focusing on minimum wage as a promise delivered and shifting to other issues that have passed the House. The ad in particular left voters underwhelmed . . . Results and meaningful change in their own lives are what matter, and they just haven't seen enough of that yet. More importantly, these

messages didn't answer the question they raised—'why aren't more of these changes being accomplished?'

The second approach we tested was a more aggressive framework, demonstrating the Democratic commitment to change and shifting the onus for the lack of progress onto President Bush . . .

"President Bush has vetoed bills to begin withdrawing troops from Iraq and to allow greater stem cell research. He has also promised to veto Democratic bills already passed by the House or Senate to lower student loan rates, implement the homeland security recommendations of the 9/11 Commission, expand health coverage for uninsured children, and allow Medicare to negotiate lower prescription drug prices."

This message fundamentally shifted the debate in the groups, *with voters wondering why Democrats weren't including those facts in their advertising* and expressing shock that Republicans are continuing to support President Bush and to defend his vetoes . . . As one woman in Illinois asked rhetorically after hearing this message, *"Are you going to stay with Bush or are you going to get with the people?"* [italics added]

What is truly interesting is to examine principled Democratic politicians who reject this bad advice. One fine example is Senator Russ Feingold of Wisconsin. He serves a swing state, which is narrowly divided in presidential elections, and which sends Republicans as often as Democrats to the House, Senate, and governor's mansion. If any senator seemingly had good cause to equivocate, it was Feingold. Yet Russ Feingold emerged as the Democrats' leader in opposing President Bush's use of extra-constitutional doctrines cloaked in national security and his assault on civil liberties. Many of Feingold's Democratic colleagues told him how much they admired his principled leadership, yet they voted with Bush because polls and pollsters told them that the voters supported the President's defense of the homeland.

What the polls missed is that these views were often ill informed as to details and shallowly held. They missed the fact that voters admire politicians with strong principles and that the task of leadership is to make public opinion better informed. Feingold violated the conventional wisdom, and his popularity in Wisconsin only increased. Wisconsin voters have the same concerns about terrorist attack as other voters. But they are now better informed than many other citizens about the fact that civil liberties need not be sacrificed—thanks to their senior senator.

What is encouraging is this: Despite more than two decades of bad advice from "third way" advocates and "New Democrats," recent classes of Democratic senators, representatives, and governors have rejected that counsel in favor of a fuller-throated reclamation of core Democratic principles. All six of the Democrats who took back Republican senate seats in 2006 ran as resolute progressives, as did most of thirty-one Democrats who picked up Republican House seats. Likewise one of the few Democratic winners in 2004, a man named Obama.

Thus the frame of the pre-Obama era. How do you change that frame? One way is to use the power of the presidency to teach, and to affirm the uneasy feeling of ordinary people that we are indeed in a crisis. The current economic situation is surely a teachable moment. At this writing, this is not yet a crisis of general collapse on the scale of the Great Depression. But if you have lost your job or your health insurance or your purchasing power (or are at risk of losing them), or your ability to be both a good parent and a conscientious employee, it is a deep crisis for you. The job of a president is to affirm that these trials are not just private anxieties, much less personal failures, but a national disgrace amenable to national remediation.

What is the alternative frame to the one that has been drilled into the collective unconscious?

1. There is in fact a crisis facing both the economic system and working Americans.

To acknowledge that the economy is in crisis is not to be a prophet of gloom and doom. It is the first step toward accepting reality, validating what people are experiencing, and pointing the way to collective improvement. One of the worst pieces of advice peddled by pundits and strategists is the idea that the American people do not want to hear about economic problems; that most people are doing so well that it's a mistake to point out the economy's failings; that candidates need to be relentlessly upbeat.

Writing for the Democratic Leadership Council in April 2006, economist Stephen Rose contended that only a small minority of voters would support Democrats based on pocketbook concerns, and that the party should identify with society's winners. Mark Penn repeatedly counseled his clients to accentuate the positive. "Using "a 'populist' message," Penn warned in an article for the DLC, "may take advantage of corporate misconduct, but it also focuses on a negative view of the U.S. economy rather than a positive agenda for growth and opportunity. It identifies with the needs of those who consider themselves victims of the economy, not people who count themselves among its beneficiaries."

This is a bit like advising someone who is visiting a cancer patient to talk about anything but the cancer. The patient knows far better than the visitor what he or she is dealing with. And people suffering from the personal costs of a national economic crisis do not want politicians to change the subject. They want the politicians to acknowledge the reality and offer some hope.

Demos's work on strategic framing suggests that merely mentioning problems is discouraging and alienating to voters. Pollsters like Penn get that part right when they warn against sounding like Chicken Little (if the sky is falling, there is nothing to be done). But transformative leaders change the public's sense of the possible with bold solutions.

2. The private sector is a source of great dynamism, but it can sure make a mess if left to its own devices.

The subprime scandal and its spawn—the housing collapse, the credit crunch, and the current bout of stagflation—are surely the greatest teachable moment for progressives in three-quarters of a century. And if that were not enough, we have the free market's failure to provide guaranteed health insurance, or pension coverage, or even employment security. Here again, the undertow of conventional wisdom will require great presidential leadership to overcome. But in case after case, reliance on the unregulated private sector has ended in tears.

3. People's needs and economic recovery are more important right now than penny pinching.

Ironically, a perverse version of this assertion has been Republican gospel going back to Ronald Reagan. President Reagan, as well as Bush I and II, insisted that deficits didn't matter as long as the proceeds were used for tax cuts that were supposed to stimulate savings and investment. The policy failed utterly. The deficit declined only when the Clinton administration restored some taxes. Deficits skyrocketed again when Bush II succeeded in cutting taxes, mostly on the rich. However, savings and investment rates fell, despite the lower tax rates. America became increasingly reliant for its investment capital on borrowing from abroad. But this deficits-don't-matter theology liberated Republicans from their previous stance as the fiscally responsible party, leaving Democrats with the politically unenviable job of persuading voters to accept tax increases in exchange for nothing but fiscal probity.

4. Tax cuts have gone mostly gone to the top, and haven't done a thing for most Americans.

This declaration needs to be coupled not with calls for fiscal austerity but with initiatives that can actually help people's lives. In the 2006 campaign, my friend Sherrod Brown, now the junior senator from Ohio, neatly checkmated his opponent's claim that Brown was a big taxer. Republican senator Mike DeWine, then the incumbent, built much of his campaign around his support for George W. Bush's tax cuts and Brown's opposition. But Brown's TV spot hit DeWine right between the eyes with the rejoinder: "Did you get any of those tax cuts, or did they all go to Mike DeWine's wealthy friends?"—because it validated the experience of most voters.

5. Government can do great things, and it particularly needs to do great things in an economic crisis.

This assertion needs to be combined with a small number of large ideas, which will both fire the imagination and deliver practical help. Some specifics are laid out in chapter 4. These five points are the policy-wonk version. It takes a great leader to turn them into political vision.

Suppose President Obama gave a major address on America's economic situation that went something like this:

> My friends, as our nation confronts the most severe economic challenges since the Great Depression, we face a choice. There are those who believe that the best idea is just to give everyone one big refund on their government—divide it up by individual portions, in the form of tax breaks; hand it out, and encourage everyone to use their share to go buy their own health care, their own retirement plan, their own child care, their own education, and so on.

In Washington, some have promoted this idea as the Ownership Society, which is a polite way of saying you are on your own. It allows us to say to those whose health care or tuition rises faster than they can afford—tough luck. It allows us to say to workers who have lost their job—life isn't fair. It lets us say to the child who was born into poverty, or the worker who lost his job because the plant moved to Mexico—pull yourself up by your bootstraps.

But this vision won't work. It ignores our history. It ignores the fact that it's been government research and investment that made the railways possible and the Internet possible; government helped create a massive middle class, through decent wages and benefits and public schools that allowed us all to prosper. Yes, our economic dependence depended partly on individual initiative; but it has also depended on our sense of mutual regard, the idea that everybody has a stake in the country, that we're all in it together and everybody's got a shot at opportunity. That's what's produced our unrivaled political stability.

But if we do nothing in the face of recession and globalization, more people will continue to lose their health care. Fewer kids will be able to afford college. More companies will be unable to provide pensions for their employees. More workers will find themselves in the unemployment line—alongside any worker whose skills can be bought and sold on the global market.

So let's dream. Instead of doing nothing or simply defending twentieth-century solutions, let's imagine together what we could do to give every American a fighting chance in the twenty-first.

What if we prepared every child in America with the education and skills they need to compete in the new economy? If we made sure that college was affordable for everyone who wanted to go? If we pledged to workers hurt by outsourcing: "Your old job is not coming back, but a new job will be there, with even better wages, because we're going to seriously retrain you and there's lifelong education that's waiting for you"?

What if no matter where you worked or how many times you switched jobs, you had health care and a pension that stayed with you always, so you all had the flexibility to move to a better job or start a new business? What if instead of cutting budgets for research and development and science, we fueled the genius and the innovation that will lead to the new jobs and new industries of the future?

What if we started with those investments that can make America more competitive in the global economy, while providing good jobs at home—investments in science and technology, and energy independence, as well as education? Ever since 1862, when Lincoln signed the Morrill Act and created the system of land-grant colleges, government has helped institutions of higher learning to serve as the nation's primary research-and-development laboratories. The federal government has provided critical support for this research infrastructure—everything from chemical labs to particle accelerators to the breakthroughs produced by the Defense Advanced Research Projects Agency, or DARPA, which underwrote the basic research that led to bar codes, the Internet, and computer-aided design, and much more.

Our current situation demands that we take the same approach with energy. We use 25 percent of the world's oil, and we can't drill our way out of the problem. A large portion of the trillion dollars that we will spend this year on imported oil, worsening our trade imbalance, goes to support some of the world's most volatile and undemocratic regimes. We can use that same government-led ingenuity that put a man on the moon and created the Internet to produce energy independence, based on renewables. And along the way we can create millions of good domestic jobs.

There's something else that government needs to do. It needs to make sure that speculative financial markets will never again push the economy into a severe and needless recession. The American experiment has worked in large part because we have guided the market's invisible hand with a higher principle. Our free market was never meant to be a free license to take whatever you can get, however you can get it. That is why we have put in place rules of the road to make competition fair, and open, and honest. We have done this not to stifle— but rather to advance prosperity and liberty. The core of our economic success is the fundamental truth that each American does better when all Americans do better; when the well-being of American business, its capital markets, and the American people are aligned.

We've lost that sense of shared prosperity, and this loss has not happened by accident. It's because of decisions made in boardrooms, on trading floors, and in Washington. Under Republican and Democratic administrations, we failed to guard against practices that all too often rewarded financial manipulation instead of productivity and sound business practices. We let the special interests put their thumbs on the economic scales. The result has been a distorted market that creates bubbles instead of steady, sustainable growth; a market that favors Wall Street over Main Street, but ends up hurting both.

The American economy does not stand still, and neither should the rules that govern it. Unfortunately, instead of establishing a twenty-first-century regulatory framework, we simply dismantled the old one. We

encouraged a winner-take-all, anything-goes environment that helped foster devastating dislocations in our
economy. And not just in financial markets.

Deregulation of the telecommunications sector, for
example, fostered competition but also contributed
to massive over-investment. Partial deregulation of
the electricity sector enabled market manipulation,
which gouged consumers and left nobody responsible
for adequate investment in the nation's power grid.
Companies like Enron and WorldCom took advantage
of the new regulatory environment to push the envelope,
pump up earnings, disguise losses, and otherwise engage
in accounting fraud to make their profits look better—a
practice that led investors to question the balance sheet
of all companies, and severely damaged public trust in
capital markets. This was not the invisible hand at work.
Instead, it was the hand of industry lobbyists tilting the
playing field in Washington, an accounting industry
that had developed powerful conflicts of interest, and a
financial sector that fueled over-investment.

Since then, we have overseen twenty-first-century
innovation—including the aggressive introduction of
new and complex financial instruments like hedge funds
and nonbank financial companies—with outdated twentieth-century regulatory tools. New conflicts of interest
recalled the worst excesses of the past. Not surprisingly,
the regulatory environment failed to keep pace. When
subprime mortgage lending took a reckless and unsustainable turn, a patchwork of regulations were unable or
unwilling to protect the American people.

How do we repair the damage? Government needs
to protect markets from their own myopia, and thereby
protect American consumers, workers, and investors.
Government needs to act to restore economic opportunity and security. With government in the hands of

those who believe in its potential for good, I pledge to you that this will be the central commitment of my administration.

Now, I am not auditioning for the job of speechwriter, so who am I to put words in the mouth of the most gifted political leader to come along in a generation? I am happy to report that these are not my words. Except for a little nipping and tucking, these are Barack Obama's words, taken from a medley of his speeches and writings.

So Obama clearly has both the rhetorical skills and the political convictions to restore popular faith in government as an instrument of collective purpose. But affirmative government requires resources as well as popular support. Given the immense undertow of conservative ideology and bad policy advice, he will need to maximize every opportunity to restore faith in what we can only do together, using government as the instrument of our common destiny.

| four |

Repairing a Damaged Economy

Make no small plans. They have no magic to stir men's
blood.

— DANIEL BURNHAM

When Barack Obama takes office as America's forty-fourth
president, he will face an acute, three-pronged economic
challenge. The financial system will be in crisis to a greater degree
than at any time since 1933. America's international imbalances
will be on a worsening downward slide. And the economy will be in
a deepening recession supercharged by falling consumer purchasing
power, declining housing values, and cascading business losses.

In addition, he faces four chronic problems that recession will
only intensify. The recession will exacerbate a thirty-year trend of
increasing inequality and insecurity. The crisis in energy and climate
change will be deepening; the unreliability and cost of health care
will be relentlessly worsening. The decay of America's public spaces
and facilities will persist. All of this will require a more activist use
of government than we've seen in at least four decades.

As we saw in chapter 3, real obstacles to change are compounded
by attitudinal ones. Assuming that he is not disabled by an undertow of dubious counsel, what exactly should Obama do? He will
have no shortage of advice, much of it contradictory, and the risk
will be either to aim too low or to run off in several directions at
once before having a clear strategic plan.

At every step, he needs to restore confidence—not just with
inspiring words or grand aspirations, but by demonstrating that
help is on the way. He also needs to transform prevailing ideo-

logical assumptions, so that the practical help attracts wide support and builds public approval for even bolder measures using activist government that will take longer to enact—and to reclaim support for the more fundamental progressive idea that government plays a constructive and necessary role.

In Roosevelt's famous First Hundred Days, FDR launched dozens of initiatives. Within just over three months, fifteen pieces of landmark legislation had passed Congress and remade the relationship between economy and government.

Obama does not need to match that record. But at the outset of his first term, he does need to address the economic emergency on three tracks. Longer-term reforms such as universal health insurance can come a little later.

First, Treasury Secretary Paulson's policy of ad hoc financial bailouts needs to be turned into a more systematic program, with explicit principles of prudential regulation. The recapitalization of America's damaged financial system must continue, perhaps at an expanded scale. But it needs to be part of a coherent strategy for restoring a sound financial system—one that the Bush administration has been incapable of creating. Second, since the housing collapse is so central both to the damaged condition of America's credit markets and to falling consumer demand, Obama needs to work with Congress on a much more robust housing and mortgage rescue program. The Frank-Dodd mortgage refinancing law and Fannie Mae–Freddie Mac guarantee enacted in late July was not a bad start, but it is not enough to do the job. And third, we will need a dramatic expansion of public spending, well into the hundreds of billions of dollars, as classic anti-depression medicine.

Begin with Low-Hanging Fruit

Obama's earliest measures should be devoted to delivering practical help to individuals, families, and communities. That will both relieve economic suffering and establish him as a leader, as well as moderate the recession. By spring 2009, we will need an immediate recovery package in the range of $200 to $300 billion, and not primarily in the form of tax cuts. That money will be needed to extend unemployment benefits; deliver money to states and localities whose falling revenues cause them to cut services in a recession; and provide the first installment on a long-term effort to rebuild public infrastructure, with an emphasis on both deferred basic maintenance and efficient renewable energy. Such public outlays can also speed development of technologies that will improve America's competitiveness and provide such twenty-first-century basics as universal broadband service.

The public works funds could be combined with an increase in job training subsidies to reduce bottlenecks in the supply of skilled workers. For example, retrofitting homes and offices for energy efficiency, building on pilot programs already operating in some small cities, could be a quick source both of good jobs and local economic stimulus. This would also yield savings on America's energy bill—which would reduce our trade imbalance and put more money in consumers' pockets.

As of early August, when this book was going to press, Obama has offered three versions of this kind of public outlay, each getting bolder as the crisis has deepened. In a speech last April, he included:

> A National Infrastructure Reinvestment Bank that will invest $60 billion over ten years and generate millions of new jobs. We can't keep standing by while our roads and bridges and airports crumble and decay. We can't keep running our economy on debt. For our economy, our safety, and our workers, we have to rebuild America.
>
> And we need to invest in green technology. We can't keep sending billions of dollars to foreign nations because of our addiction to oil. We should be investing in American companies that invest in American-manufactured solar panels and windmills, and in clean coal technology.

> That's why I've proposed investing $150 billion over the next ten years in the green energy sector.

This is exactly what's needed, but the scale should be bigger. Later he proposed a second stimulus package of $50 billion, of which $30 billion was to be tax cuts. That was far too feeble.

Then, on July 31, after his economic summit meeting and the Labor Department's announcement of higher unemployment, came stronger medicine. Obama proposed $25 billion for a "State Growth Fund to prevent state and local cuts in health, education and housing assistance or counterproductive increases in property taxes, tolls or fees." The fund would also fund home heating and weatherization assistance. Second, he proposed another $25 billion for a Jobs and Growth Fund to replenish the highway trust fund, prevent cutbacks in road and bridge maintenance, and fund new fast-tracked projects to repair schools. All of this, he said, would "save more than 1 million jobs in danger of being cut."

This proposal was a welcome down payment on an idea that progressives have been proposing for three decades—a "ready-to-go" program of standby anti-recession investment in public infrastructure. The idea is that localities can qualify in advance for preapproved projects, which can then be launched on relatively short notice. When recession strikes, the federal government would release the funds, with the money divided among localities according to a formula. With the economy in serious trouble and a $1.6 trillion infrastructure backlog, this program is probably necessary for several years, and should be continued as an ongoing standby measure.

In the first phase, federal public works outlay could begin delivering badly needed public funds and decent jobs within as little as ninety days—money to repair and refurbish roads, bridges, mass transit, parks, schools, and public buildings, or to prevent cuts in state and local budgets. Gearing up a planning system for a more expansive second phase should take about six months. During the Depression, Roosevelt got money flowing in a matter of weeks. Later, the Public Works Administration not only delivered tangible public improvements and good jobs but also created a local planning system in which proposed projects were discussed and debated by citizens, who played a role in setting local priorities.

Why begin here? Three big reasons. First, this approach would deliver tangible, visible help, and quickly. Second, it would be politically irresistible—for the very reason that conservative opponents of public outlay love to hate: It would have elements of what is disparaged as pork-barrel spending. Every congressional district would get its share (would you like to be the congressman who voted against such a measure in a serious recession?). Harder-hit regions of the country would qualify for extra aid.

Third, an economic downturn supercharged by a credit contraction is a different creature from an ordinary business-cycle recession. About 16 percent of America's homes have mortgages worth more than the value of the house. As economic activity slows, business defaults are rising. Loans that would be considered perfectly sound in normal times are being turned down or charged higher interest costs, because panicky banks have suddenly turned risk-averse. When businesses and consumers have trouble getting credit, economic activity slows and recession becomes a self-fulfilling prophecy. We saw this first in the subprime collapse, which gradually spread to the entire banking sector, and then to the rest of the economy. As a consequence, public spending needs to do heavier lifting than usual to counteract the depressive effect of a credit crunch.

Yes, Deficits

In the short run, part of this program of public works would be deficit-financed, as Obama recognized in moving beyond an earlier and ill-advised promise last spring that all his new spending programs would be offset by cuts elsewhere. It is a matter of basic macroeconomics that new outlays that are offset by other budget cuts or tax increases provide no net stimulus. After Obama announced his emergency anti-recession program on July 31, he gave an interview to NPR's usually intelligent Michele Norris. Norris, in a flawless rendition of the conventional wisdom, asked in a slightly horrified tone, "This morning you announced a new emergency economic plan. It includes a $50 billion package. Can you promise to pay for all that without increasing our debt? Where will this money come from?"

Obama explained, "When it comes to a stimulus package, typically you are not looking at offsets, because what you are trying to do is to prevent the economy from going into a further tailspin."

But Norris persisted with the usual story: "But with the deficit as high as it is right now, is it responsible to propose something that is likely to increase deficit spending?"

Obama didn't flinch: "Well, Michele," he said, "understand that if we continue on the trends we're on right now, where unemployment keeps on going up—I'm in Florida, where they are in recession for the first time in 16 years—if you continue to see an economic slide, that is going to cost far more in terms of tax revenues, because businesses aren't selling, taxes aren't being collected. And what we're going to end up with is a much worse situation when it comes to our deficit."

This exchange occurred during a week when McCain was closing the polling gap with Obama and Democrats were expressing alarm that Obama had not yet made the sale with enough white working-class voters despite worsening economic conditions that should play to Democratic advantage. By explaining the stakes and offering tangible help, Obama positioned himself to be an effective president—as well as increasing the odds that he would reach the White House at all.

In the financial collapse of the Great Depression, Roosevelt turned to previously unknown peacetime deficit spending of around 4 to 6 percent of GDP. It turned out that this level of pump priming was necessary but not sufficient to fully restore prosperity. On the eve of the wartime mobilization, unemployment had been cut only in half, from a peak of 25 percent to about 12 percent. The economy kept slipping back into recessions. Full recovery came only with the even greater deficit-financed government spending of World War II, which peaked at 30 percent of GDP.

We are not in another Great Depression, and we don't need a recovery program on the scale of World War II. But we will need increased deficits, at least for a year or two until we are on the road to recovery. Even if we did nothing, the recession itself would reduce economic activity, hence tax receipts, and only an economic idiot (or perhaps the International Monetary Fund) counsels fiscal austerity in a deep recession.

A temporary increase in deficit spending might offend Democratic budgetary conservatives who have embraced pay-as-you-go budget rules both on grounds of fiscal prudence and as a defensive strategy against further Republican tax cutting. Under these so-called pay-go rules, all new outlays and all new tax cuts need to be "paid for," either by other program cuts or other tax increases. For example, in the first stimulus package, a rather meager $168 billion affair passed by Congress last February, conservative Blue Dog Democrats joined far-right Republicans in blocking a more expansive measure because they didn't support increasing the deficit. But as Obama explained so cogently, the very definition of a fiscal stimulus is a temporary increase in deficit spending.

At the same time, not all stimulus programs are fiscal. For the longer term, there is a good argument that raising taxes on the very wealthy and spending the money on old-fashioned public works or investments in energy independence, science and technology, or college aid would have a net stimulative effect, even if the deficit impact were neutral. The reason is that every penny would be spent, whereas the nontaxed incomes of the very wealthy might be saved, moved abroad, or invested in nonproductive uses such as diamonds, gold, or pre-Columbian art.

Legislatively, I am assuming that while an emergency public

works program was advancing on one track, a program to repeal the Bush tax cuts would be moving on another. There might or might not be an exact rendezvous. But pay-as-you-go budgeting was a tactic for another era, one in which Republican tax give-aways needed to be restrained, and one in which the economy was not in deepening recession. Fiscally, as FDR belatedly recognized, budget rules that make sense for normal times do not apply in an economic emergency. Over the entire business cycle, fairly moderate deficits of, say, 2 percent of GDP are sensible. But in a severe recession, greater deficit spending makes sense; and in no event should a public works program be held hostage to a balanced budget, much less to long-term reform of social insurance.

Beyond an immediate and more expansive program to increase jobs and fiscal relief for communities, the new administration will need to move on multiple fronts. Here again, the most important principle is first to do what needs to be done to stop the bleeding while building toward more expansive successes in the future.

The Special Case of Housing

By July 2008, there were 272,171 foreclosures recorded, a 55-percent increase from a year earlier. Homeowners were losing trillions of dollars of home equity, the principal form of their net worth. During the boom years, as incomes lagged behind inflation but housing values surpassed it, homeowners got into the habit of borrowing against their homes. By spring 2008, more than half of the value of America's homes was not equity but debt, up from just 20 percent debt in the 1960s; it was the worst debt-to-equity ratio since World War II. Plummeting housing values contributed to the downward spiral of reduced consumer spending and shrunken economic activity generally.

The Frank-Dodd housing bill, enacted and signed (with no ceremony) by a reluctant President Bush in late July, included provisions enabling people stuck with subprime loans at astronomical interest rates to get refinancing at more modest interest costs, with the loans guaranteed by FHA. But there will be a great deal of litigation on whether a holder of the loan is obligated to accept the refinancing. The Congressional Budget Office estimates that only about 400,000 homes will be refinanced over the next three years thanks to the bill. Yet 2 to 3 million homeowners are expected to default on their mortgages in 2008 alone.

CBO also calculated that the banks are likely to off-load the riskiest loans onto FHA, and that 35 percent of these lower-interest-rate mortgages will eventually default, at taxpayer expense. In the end, the rescue program could do more to help banks than homeowners, according to CBO. In fairness, the whole point of the bill was to refinance the mortgages at great risk of foreclosure. The problem is that the bill, by itself, solves only a fraction of the problem.

A more expansive provision of the Democrats' bill would have included upward of $10 billion to enable local governments and nonprofit agencies to buy foreclosed-upon houses and either return them to the rental housing supply or sell them with low-interest-rate mortgages to moderate-income buyers. The Bush administration and fiscally conservative Blue Dog Democrats in the House blocked this provision as adding to the deficit. (What are they waiting for—a full-blown depression?)

The next version of the housing and mortgage rescue program will need to be far bolder. Only presidential leadership can accomplish that. Once again, the New Deal offers a precedent.

Before the Roosevelt era, virtually all mortgages were short-term loans of five years of less, typically interest-only, with the principal due and payable at the end. If homeowners could not roll over the loan, they were out of luck. As foreclosures skyrocketed in the early 1930s, the New Deal invented the modern long-term, self-amortizing mortgage. The government offered to insure such mortgages so that lenders would accept them, devising the Federal National Mortgage Administration (FNMA) to create a "secondary market" to purchase mortgages from lenders, turn them into government bonds, and replenish the bank's money so that the banker could make more loans.

As foreclosures kept rising because of the general economic conditions, Roosevelt and Congress also created the Home Owners Loan Corporation, which made low-interest direct loans at the government's own borrowing rate. Eventually, HOLC refinanced one American home in five, saving innumerable families from foreclosure, reviving a normal market in real estate, and tempering the free fall in housing prices. Because there was no corruption and loan standards were maintained, when HOLC closed its doors in 1952, it returned a modest profit to the Treasury.

There is surely a lesson here—which could usefully be the subject of another Obama teachable moment. When people who believe in government operate it competently, the public sector can often outperform the private, particularly when the purpose is partly social. Under the New Deal schema of financial regulation, which suffered its first serious assaults only in the late 1970s, there were no major banking scandals or losses. FNMA performed beautifully, and mortgage credit was plentiful. The rate of homeownership rose from 44 percent in 1940 to 64 percent by the mid-1960s. Only after FNMA was privatized as Fannie Mae, and its executives began paying themselves multimillion-dollar salaries and taking exotic financial risks, did the institution get into big trouble.

The July 2008 housing legislation, though useful, will prove far too weak to halt the epidemic of foreclosures and the collapse in real estate values. Before this housing collapse is over, government will need something like a Home Owners Loan Corporation with the power to refinance mortgages when the private market fails. The agency should have a separate window to underwrite efforts by local government to get foreclosed houses reoccupied so that they don't drag down entire neighborhoods. This strategy could be part of a long-overdue need to subsidize affordable housing. This or something like it will need to be enacted in Obama's first hundred days. As congressmen and senators hear from constituents about collapsing housing values, dwindling real estate tax receipts, and devastated homebuilding firms, this bill should be among Obama's easier legislative challenges.

In recent years, the private housing market has seen the coexistence of feast and famine. Part of it was a bubble economy that produced windfall gains for some and ultimately invited a crash. Elsewhere, as rents followed prices upward and conservative administrations withdrew subsidies for affordable housing, tens of millions of people were paying more than a third of their incomes for shelter. Many more were doubling up or enduring two-hour commutes to work from distant small towns where prices were still relatively low.

The housing crisis creates an opportunity for government to connect millions of foreclosed-upon houses with millions of aspiring homeowners and renters seeking affordable shelter. The missing ingredient is subsidized mortgages and creative community lenders. A bold program along these lines would brake the slide in housing prices by subsidizing the purchasing power of new occupants.

One of the many perverse things about the subprime industry was that it advertised itself as the friend of moderate-income homeowners. But by offering them bait-and-switch loans with teaser rates that soon reset to interest rates that might make the Mafia blush, these lenders robbed people of their dreams. If we want to help people of modest means acquire homes, the proven way is not to charge exorbitant rates but to use subsidized mortgages with below-market rates, coupled with counseling. There are plenty of proven models, such as the fine work of Shorebank of Chicago, near Obama's old neighborhood, or Neighborhood Housing Services, both of which help moderate-income Americans realize secure homeownership. All that's lacking is adequate federal subsidy.

For the more complex reform projects of the new administration—restoring a secure financial system; revising trade priorities; expanding the supply of good jobs; devising a path to secure renewable energy; moving toward universal health insurance—it makes sense for the new administration to take some months to plan, and then to build support in the country. Task forces in each area could tender reports while the emergency business of stopping a slide toward depression proceeds.

Rebuilding Secure Financial Markets

In the current financial collapse, all of the complex, separate abuses that caused the current crisis really boiled down to three: too much speculation with borrowed money; too little transparency and disclosure; and too many insider conflicts of interest. These abuses, in turn, were the bitter fruit of deregulation. The parallels to similar abuses of the 1920s are exact.

All of these abuses will need to be remedied. We did precisely that as part of the New Deal. But beginning in the 1970s, much of the New Deal system of financial regulation was repealed in the name of more modern and innovative markets that supposedly did not need government. By 2000, a clean, transparent financial system that had made American capital markets the envy of the world was destroyed. The business geniuses who brought America this wisdom are now humbled by events. Their allies and enablers among financial economists based convoluted theories on the general premise that financial markets were entirely self-correcting. These economists are roughly in the position of pre-Copernican astronomers who hung elaborate models on the premise that the sun revolved around the earth. They should seek honest employment.

Former Federal Reserve chairman Paul Volcker, in a high-profile address to the Economic Club of New York last April, put it well:

> We have moved from a commercial bank centered, highly regulated financial system, to an enormously more complicated and highly engineered system. Today, much of the

financial intermediation takes place in markets beyond effective official oversight and supervision, all enveloped in unknown trillions of derivative instruments. It has been a highly profitable business, with finance accounting recently for 35 to 40 percent of all corporate profits.

It is hard to argue that the new system has brought exceptional benefits to the economy generally. Economic growth and productivity in the last 25 years has been comparable to that of the 1950's and 60's, but in the earlier years the prosperity was more widely shared.

In the last months of the lame-duck Bush administration, however, something very odd happened. As the situation became more dire, with threats to the largest banks and to mortgage giants Fannie Mae and Freddie Mac, as well as the looming risk of a general financial collapse, Treasury Secretary Henry Paulson became a reluctant paladin of big government. Paulson had assumed office in June 2006 with an agenda of further financial deregulation. In the months after he joined the cabinet, there was a well-coordinated flurry of activity with reports by conservative task forces all pointing to the evils of financial regulation, including a Committee on Capital Markets Regulation chaired by Paulson himself. That body's report, released in November 2006, recommended several steps toward regulatory weakening in the name of greater competitiveness.

However, by the time Paulson issued a follow-up report in March 2008 on behalf of a resurrected President's Working Group on Financial Markets, reality had overtaken his design. In mid-2007, credit markets had suddenly frozen because of fallout from the subprime collapse. The Federal Reserve had to advance hundreds of billions of dollars to banks to keep credit flowing. So Paulson's 2008 report was a thoroughly contradictory overlay of two documents—one expressing his earlier dogma praising the genius of unregulated markets, the other promoting government rescue and promising stricter supervision of large banks that posed systemic risks.

Thus did the champion of deregulation become the leader of a squad tasked with cleaning up the mess deregulation had made. Paulson, improvising as he went along, offered a deus ex machina as his counterweight to further deregulation. He proposed to give the Federal Reserve yet-to-be-defined blanket authority to monitor the largest commercial and investment banks, to make sure that none were posing excessive risks to the system. The trouble with this approach is that by the time a large institution shows signs of distress, it is far too late.

As the crisis deepened, Paulson at the Treasury and Ben Bernanke at the Federal Reserve lurched from ad hoc bailout to ad hoc bailout, with no coherent regulatory theory or policy either to prevent unacceptably risky behavior before the fact, or to determine when to bail out an institution after it got into trouble. A bank deemed "too big to fail" because of the risk of spillover dangers was like Justice Potter Stewart's famous definition of pornography: You just knew it when you saw it. Indy Mac, a medium-size regional bank, was allowed to fail. But Bear Stearns, Fannie Mae, and Freddie Mac got taxpayer bailouts. In the shotgun acquisition by Citi, Bear's shareholders lost almost everything. Fannie's were partly protected. So it goes.

By August 2008, the government had brokered an emergency takeover of Bear Stearns by JPMorgan Chase at fire-sale prices, putting $29 billion of taxpayer money at risk; offered a general line of credit to large investment banks that previously enjoyed no special government guarantee or supervision; put government capital at the disposal of Fannie Mae and Freddie Mac; and invited banks and investment companies to exchange dubious paper for Treasury bills, in order to recapitalize banks and move markets in risky securities that nobody else wanted to buy. The Fed, which has about a trillion dollars at its disposal, tied up something like 40 percent of its own capital in these serial rescues.

All of this was done under the Federal Reserve's emergency authority enacted during the Roosevelt administration. With the exception of the Fannie Mae–Freddie Mac bailout, none of it had congressional authorization, nor did the Bush administration announce an explicit reversal of the general policy of financial deregulation. All the moves had the same panicky, ad hoc character.

Now, it is a very good thing that Paulson put aside his ideological blinders and worked with Ben Bernanke and Tim Geithner at the Federal Reserve to prevent the credit freeze from becoming a complete economic collapse. But people like Paulson, former head of Goldman Sachs, want the emergency rescues without the prudential regulation. The next administration will need to combine the two strategies, as Roosevelt's did.

In the summer of 2008, a new and alarming element deepened the crisis: runs on banks, but with two twists. Deposits were insured by the Federal Deposit Insurance Corporation—a core part of the New Deal that had not been repealed during the orgy of deregulation. So there was no reason for depositors to trigger runs on banks, the traditional worry prior to creation of the FDIC. But these new runs were *shareholder* runs. As details of the crisis unfolded, it became ever clearer to investors that bank balance sheets were seriously weakened in two distinct respects.

First, these balance sheets were full of dubious securities that suddenly nobody wanted to buy. These included not just securities based on subprime loans but also other exotic forms of securitized credit backed by everything from car loans to credit cards, and even more abstruse securities that insured other securities against default. If banks followed normal accounting practices and "marked to market" securities that had no buyers and technically had a value of zero, the banks would be declared insolvent. In a credit crunch, it was this fear that caused the Fed to pump so much emergency liquidity (money) into the banking system. In fact, the agency that governs financial accounting standards moved, under pressure from the SEC and the Treasury, to scrap a rule that required banks to mark down the valuation of their assets to their current trading value (in many cases zero)—lest all the large banks be judged insolvent.

Second, much of the banks' fee and interest income had been based on underwriting or trading these very same securities, or making other highly leveraged and highly risky deals. If this lucrative line of business was suddenly no longer available, banks not only had trouble on their balance sheets in the reduced value of their assets—they also had serious problems with their earnings.

As these twin vulnerabilities became apparent and bank losses mounted, shareholders began fleeing banks. No bank was big enough to be safe. During the first seven months of 2007, when the broad stock market lost about 20 percent, the index of bank stocks went down almost by half. Some large regional banks did far worse. Cleveland-based National City Bank's stock was down 90 percent. Washington Mutual fell 76 percent. The stock of the Swiss-based global giant UBS lost 70 percent. Shares in the flagship brokerage firm Merrill Lynch lost more than half.

In the case of a commercial bank, the value of a bank's shares is a major portion of the equity against which it can lend. The other major component of bank equity is its capital reserves. As losses mounted in 2008, both forms of capital footings took a huge hit, worsening the general credit contraction.

One other factor deepened the crisis—the abuse and proliferation of "short selling." This twist also has instructive ideological implications. In selling a stock short, an investor who thinks a stock price is headed downward borrows the shares from a broker, delivers them to a purchaser, buys back the identical number of shares on the open market after the price has fallen, and then pockets the difference. This is how some investors make money in a falling market. The practice of short selling doesn't do much damage in a normal market, but organized on a large scale it can turn a bear market into a crash.

In the summer of 2008, short sellers (many of them hedge funds) smelled blood in the financial waters. They savagely bid down the price of bank stocks. Human nature being what it is, many short sellers invented or passed along rumors that exaggerated the weak condition of several large banks. Executives of

Bear Stearns blamed their demise on rumormongers and short sellers. The venerable firm of Lehman Brothers seemed headed for insolvency, pulled down by short sellers' rumors that turned out to be untrue. The same psychology threatened Fannie Mae.

The legal status of such rumor mongering is ambiguous. Short selling is permissible, but deliberately manipulating markets is a felony. Deciding when passing along a juicy rumor becomes deliberate market manipulation is a Jesuitical endeavor at best. But in July 2008, one of the most ideologically conservative Securities and Exchange Commissions since the institution was created during the New Deal did something startling. Faced with organized short-selling raids that were depressing the stocks of major financial institutions and threatening their very solvency, the SEC rushed out an emergency thirty-day order warning that it would be on the lookout for short-selling abuses against the shares of nineteen flagship financial firms, and would vigorously go after violators. The order prohibited new short sales of shares in such wounded giants as Lehman Brothers, Merrill Lynch, Citigroup, Fannie Mae, and Bank of America unless the seller had already borrowed the stock. Christopher Cox, one of the most anti-regulation ideologues ever to chair the SEC, boasted, "There have long been clear rules in place that prohibit market manipulation. But for the entirety of its 74-year history until 2008, the Commission has never brought an enforcement action of this kind."

Behind this surprising turnabout hangs a tale. Reformers have actually been trying to ban short selling since the late 1920s. For generations, however, conventional financial economists have defended short selling as helping to lubricate the efficient functioning of markets. Anyone who argued that short selling was needless mischief that did nothing for the real economy was ridiculed as a hopeless radical.

In fact, the original design of Franklin Roosevelt's 1934 securities legislation recognized the hazards of short selling and sought to ban it outright. One of the many abuses of the 1920s had been market manipulation via short selling, known as bear raids. Even before Roosevelt took office, liberal members of Congress had introduced legislation to either discourage short selling by collecting windfall taxes on the proceeds, or simply prohibit it.

The Securities Exchange Act of 1934, policing the conduct of stock exchanges and creating the Securities and Exchange Commission, was the object of fierce battles between progressives and conservatives in the Congress and the country. The draft bill included a flat ban on short selling as well as other abuses that came back to haunt financial markets in the past two decades—excessive leverage, conflicts of interest, and favored treatment of insiders. But by the time the Wall Street lobbies got finished with the bill—enlisting small-town bankers and national networks of retail stockbrokers as their allies—all these teeth had been removed.

For eight decades, short selling has been part of the financial landscape. It is a mark of just how dire are current conditions that in 2008 a panicky and conservative SEC that doesn't much believe in regulation embraced an ad hoc remedy that had eluded even Roosevelt. The fact that Wall Street, at the nadir of its disgrace in 1933, still had the clout to block these reforms suggests something of the residual power that the Obama administration will be up against.

The men and women currently in charge of the executive branch, deep believers in laissez-faire, have no coherent theory of financial regulation, so their separate emergency measures lack policy coherence. In their hearts, they oppose what they are being compelled to do in a crisis. And so we still have a system that privatizes speculative gain and socializes the risks. Obama, unlike Bush, will have an entirely different cast of cabinet and regulatory officials as well as technical experts, all of whom presumably believe in the enterprise of regulation.

Criteria for prudent regulation need to rebuilt from the ground up. The core principle is that any financial institution that creates credit (and thereby creates risks that could undermine the system) needs to be subjected to the same kind of regulatory criteria—whether that institution calls itself a bank, a mortgage company, an investment bank, a hedge fund, or a private equity firm. Indeed, if Congress were to extend requirements on capital adequacy, leverage, and greater transparency from commercial banks to investment banks, Goldman Sachs (a very lightly regulated investment bank) would turn itself into a hedge fund. And if Congress extended prudential requirements to hedge funds, Goldman would become a private equity company.

The point is that these financial firms increasingly all do the same kinds of things. And they buy and sell products with one another, many of them poorly understood, highly speculative, and sometimes toxic; it all goes into the same financial bloodstream. Last year, about 60 percent of the credit created in the United States was created by lightly regulated firms other than depository institutions. As Barack Obama grasped so well in his Cooper Union speech, which I quoted in chapter 1, "We need to regulate institutions for what they do, not what they are."

As he declared in that speech last March, when many Democrats were still rather timid about confronting the ideology of deregulation head-on,

> There needs to be general reform of the requirements to which all regulated financial institutions are subjected. Capital requirements should be strengthened, particularly for complex financial instruments like some of the mortgage securities that led to our current crisis. We must develop and rigorously manage liquidity risk. We must investigate rating agencies and potential conflicts of interest with the people they are rating. And transparency requirements must demand full disclosure by financial institutions to shareholders and counterparties.

It logically follows that some entire categories of financial transactions and instruments need to be banned as adding more risks than benefits. We should revisit the old arguments about short selling. There is a strong case that the abuses outweigh any benefits. We should reconsider the original draft of Roosevelt's securities legislation, which proposed to make it illegal for members of stock exchanges to trade for their own accounts as an inherent conflict of interest with their arm's-length service to their customers. We need to investigate the inherent conflict of interest in the stock exchanges' specialist system, in which traders can also profit by trading ahead of their customers.

Bond rating agencies, as presently constructed, display multiple conflicts of interest. They are paid by originators of securities for consulting work to enable those securities to earn a triple-A rating—bestowed by the same bond rating agencies. Had these agencies operated at arm's length, bonds based on subprime mortgage loans would have fetched few buyers. The bond rating companies, which do business with firms that insure securities against default, systematically punish municipal bonds with lower ratings than comparable private-sector bonds to help the insurance firms capture fees. The whole system would be more efficient and transparent if bond rating were vested in a public or nonprofit institution, whose costs could be covered by a very small fee on all financial transactions.

We need to recall and reclaim the fundamental purpose of credit and capital markets—channeling funds from investors to entrepreneurs. The whole business has become riddled with middlemen who invent complex products that add little to the efficiency of credit markets, magnify systemic risks, and mainly serve to line their own pockets and corrupt their confederates.

Supervision needs to be tightened across the board, and not just of the largest institutions, based on explicit criteria of safety and prudence. This approach could not be ventured by the Bush administration, both because the clock ran out and because it was considered an ideological abomination. Reconstructing principles of financial regulation will fall to Obama.

In making the case for a reversal of ideology and practice, Obama needs to help the public grasp the astonishing double standard in current policy. Trillions of dollars of help are going to bail out the nation's wealthiest speculators and the financial institutions that they put at risk of collapse. The usual rules are waived for these emergency bailouts, while tens of millions of ordinary Americans suffering from these abuses get little or nothing. As John Bogle, founder of Vanguard Group of mutual funds and the rare Wall Street statesman, aptly put it, "The banks are too big to fail and the man in the street is too small to bail."

There is also an international dimension to restoration of effective financial regulation. Many hedge funds and private equity firms are registered offshore in regulatory havens that provide even less regulation than the feeble scrutiny such firms get in the United States. If we are going to apply Obama's principle that we must "regulate institutions for what they do, not what they are," then there can't be an all-purpose loophole for those domiciled offshore. This is not as difficult as it sounds. All it would take is a rule that any financial firm that does business with a bank operating in the United States must be subjected to a level of scrutiny equal to that of domestic firms. Many of our trading partners, nations whose economies are suffering grave harm because of a financial crisis created in the United States, would welcome this regulatory toughening.

Obama needs to define the moment. And he needs to begin anew. Presumably, he will assemble the best minds—a set of advisers who have an entirely different conception of the necessary role of financial regulation—and reclaim a theory of market failure based on the potent evidence of recent events. Here, too, Obama will have to fight an undertow, for much of the deregulation that spawned the current financial disaster dates to the Clinton administration. The Clinton Treasury Department was headed by Robert Rubin, a fervent believer in deregulation, who provides Obama with occasional advice and who is cited as a wise counsel in *The Audacity of Hope*. Even Rubin, however, is singing something of a different tune after the credit collapse.

Obama's administration will need to sort which practices must be prohibited outright as inherently prone to abuse, and which should be subject to exactly what sort of tighter regulation, and by which new or old government agencies. Only then can he send Congress legislation to implement policy. And along the way, he needs to rely on his gift as a teacher—as Roosevelt did in the banking crisis of 1933, and Obama himself did so brilliantly in his Cooper Union address.

However, turning around public and congressional opinion on the subject of financial regulation will be no mean feat. Wall Street welcomes the bailouts; it still resists the regulation. A massive job of public education will be required. Before this financial crisis ends, the government may well end up recapitalizing America's banks. One could fairly say that the process has already begun, piecemeal, based on the ad hoc bailouts orchestrated by Secretary Paulson and the Federal Reserve. We have been here before, but with a difference. In the 1930s, Roosevelt's Reconstruction Finance Corporation recapitalized many banks and corporations. But the difference was this: On a parallel track, the New Deal was also building a modern system of financial regulation to spare future generations the pattern of speculation, crash, and bailout. This is now the historic task of the Obama administration. It should not have been necessary a second time.

Good Jobs at Good Wages

The theme of well-paying jobs and good career horizons has been part of every Democratic platform and every major speech on the economy in our political lifetimes. But virtually all of the proposals in the political mainstream are too feeble to alter a stubborn thirty-year trend.

On top of engineering a recovery from severe recession, Obama needs to reverse the broader pattern of increasing insecurity and inequality if he is to make a mark as a great president and win decisive reelection. Otherwise we will survive the financial collapse only to continue on a path that shortchanges most Americans. Transformative is precisely the word to describe what needs to be done.

For better than three decades, good jobs with secure careers have become more elusive—except for the 4 percent of people with advanced degrees. We surely need a better-educated population; but as the economist Frank Levy has observed, the answer to stagnant wage trends is not to get everybody an MBA or a law degree. In the twenty-five years prior to 1973, salaries and wages increased in lockstep with rising productivity growth. Ordinary workers, without exceptional levels of educational attainment, could look forward to secure jobs and rising incomes over their life course. In fact, despite pervasive racial and sex discrimination, the overall distribution of household income was far more equal in 1958 than in 2008.

Productivity growth dipped in the 1970s and 1980s, and a lot of economists blamed the stagnant wages on the slower productivity growth. Productivity gains came roaring back in the 1990s and 2000s, the fruit of the computer revolution—but earnings only became more unequal and jobs less secure.

Before we can understand how to reverse this trend, we need a clear understanding of what occurred. Basically, workers prior to the mid-1970s enjoyed far more bargaining power to get their fair share of the pie. Unions were stronger; measures such as more generous minimum-wage regulation and unemployment compensation enhanced workers' ability to get their share. More industries were regulated, giving companies a stable rate of return and far less incentive to hammer down wages as a strategy of price competition. Large and stable firms could extend greater security to their employees. And America was largely insulated from low-wage global competition. All of this was anchored in a different conception of a more managed form of capitalism and a different politics.

Some of the trends that have increased worker insecurity, as Obama has correctly pointed out, cannot be reversed. The large, stable corporation is gone forever, as is America's unique economic dominance during a period when Europe was still recovering from war and Asia had not yet joined the modern global economy. Yet there are plenty of available remedies that public policy has avoided, because of either cost, or ideological opposition, or both—strategies that can offset these structural changes to the economy and restore a more balanced form of capitalism.

There is no more effective force for decent wages and working conditions than the labor movement. One obvious thing that Obama can do early on is to help the labor movement fight back against vicious and illegal union busting. President Roosevelt's Wagner Act, passed in 1935, guarantees workers the right to organize or join a union if they so choose. But since the early 1970s, corporate America has been increasingly brazen in its campaign to break unions. The most efficient way to do so is to fire workers who support unions, even though that is a flagrant violation of the Wagner Act. Enforcement has become so enfeebled that years go by before dismissed workers can win reinstatement or the payment of token fines and back wages. Most don't even try. Union-busting managers treat these expenses as ordinary costs of doing business.

The claim today that the decline in union membership has occurred because most workers no longer want or need unions is at odds with the evidence. Polls show that upward of 50 percent of workers who are not currently members of unions would like to join. They refrain from doing so for fear of retaliation or harassment.

Legislation to restore effective worker rights under the Wagner Act has been regularly introduced in every Congress since the early 1970s. In 1978, when Jimmy Carter enjoyed an overwhelming Democratic majority in Congress, labor law reform failed for two votes in the Senate because Carter did not lift a finger to win wavering support. In 1993–94, when Clinton had a working legislative majority, he gave priority not to a stronger Wagner Act but to NAFTA—whose main adversary was the labor movement.

The current reform legislation under consideration, the Employee Free Choice Act, would expedite the process of union certification once a majority of workers at a given worksite had signed union cards. Under present procedures, after a majority indicates that they want a union, there is a protracted period before an election during which time organizers and pro-union workers are often fired, threats are made, and management has license to wage anti-union campaigns with captive audiences. The new system would short-circuit that period of abuse and allow certification based on a majority of signed cards.

Obama has endorsed the legislation and pledged to make it an early priority. Even if he is successful in winning its enactment, however, he should prize the labor movement as a constituency to be honored and enlarged. Compared with identically situated workers in non-union settings, rank-and-file members of unions tend to have a far more progressive and socially conscious conception of the economy, more enlightened attitudes on race and gender, and a greater tendency to look to civic engagement and remedy. They and their families also have a far greater propensity to vote for Democrats.

Recent Democratic presidents have looked to the labor movement to ring doorbells, staff phone banks, and donate money, but have often viewed it merely as an interest group that requires tending rather than an anchor of the progressive coalition. Bill Clinton seated Alan Greenspan next to the first lady in the House gallery during his first State of the Union address. In that seat of honor, Obama could recognize the rank-and-file leaders of a local union who braved harassment and intimidation to win a union contract. It was John L. Lewis, in the early days of the CIO, who would tell groups of workers, "President Roosevelt wants you to join the union." Today's trade unionists should be able to say that of Barack Obama.

No matter how effectively the next administration adds labor or environmental standards to trade agreements, many millions of jobs will continue to be outsourced. Yet the fastest-growing part of the economy is the service sector—most of whose jobs need to remain close to their customers and clients. These are the very people whose daily struggles Obama listened to while he was a community organizer on the South Side of Chicago, and when he developed an early political alliance with the SEIU.

Having seen firsthand the successes of unions in improving the lives of janitors, security guards, nurse-aides, room cleaners in hotels, workers at the sinks in restaurant kitchens, I can report that no economic scene in America is more diverse, more noble, more civic, or more democratic than a union convention honoring workers who have just taken immense risks to organize a union that requires the humblest workers to be treated like human beings. Yes, America needs its entrepreneurs. But it surely needs its unions. Obama should lionize these American heroes, and not just at their own conventions. He should introduce them, with pride, to the rest of America. He, the nation, and his party will be rewarded.

Professionalize the Human-Service Economy

As a signature initiative, Obama could use government's broader regulatory and spending power to transform the thirty-year trend toward bad and insecure jobs. During the same three decades, the service sector has exploded as a source of employment. The American workforce has been transformed from 28 percent factory workers and 72 percent service workers in 1978 to 16 percent factory workers and 84 percent service workers today. But the service sector encompasses tens of millions of bad jobs—in routine clerical work, retail sales, fast food, low-end human services—and a relatively small number of very well-compensated professional positions, among them doctor, lawyer, scientist, and investment banker.

Even with stronger minimum-wage laws and unions, it will take a revolutionary shift to make every fast-food and checkout clerk job one that truly pays a living wage. But one thing that government could do in the meantime is exert influence in a key and growing sector where government pays most of the bills—the human services.

Suppose the new administration announced a national policy goal of converting every human-service job to a good job that pays a living wage with good benefits and includes adequate training, professional status, and the prospect of advancement—a career rather than casual labor. These, after all, are jobs caring for our parents, our children, and ourselves. Transforming all human-service work into good jobs would not merely replenish the supply of decent work. It would vastly improve the quality of care delivered to the elderly at home or in institutions; to young children in pre-kindergartens or day-care facilities; and to sick people whether in hospitals, hospices, outpatient settings, or their homes.

These are also, quintessentially, the jobs that cannot be outsourced. Even if we succeed in reviving American manufacturing, the process of automation means that America is almost certain to become even more of a service economy over time. Good service-sector jobs can help replace good factory jobs.

Many economists once thought that widening income inequality was caused in part by this shift to a service economy, where average productivity was both lower and more static over time. Factory jobs, the argument went, tended to pay above the median wage because each job added a lot of value. The more productive and capital-intensive the machinery became over time, the more value each job added. So by the mid–twentieth century, industrial workers could command middle-class wages and good fringe benefits. By contrast, human-service jobs were hands-on and labor-intensive. A nursing-home worker or a pre-k teacher was low-tech. So the pay was low, too.

We now know that this picture was highly misleading. How do we know? Just look at the global economy. Autoworkers in Mexico use the same production technology as workers in Michigan, but their pay is about $2 an hour. In China, autoworkers may earn $2 a day. It turns out that American autoworkers were paid middle-class wages not because of something inherent about making cars but because the United Auto Workers had the power to negotiate good wages. Conversely, Scandinavia has no low-wage human-service workers because it has made a decision that everyone who takes care of the sick, the old, or the young is a professional or at least a paraprofessional and is compensated as such.

Since most human-service costs are paid socially, choices about how to compensate workers are social decisions, not purely ones of private supply and demand. In the United States, with our meager social outlay, we define these positions as low-wage, casual jobs. In the Nordic countries, the people who work in pre-kindergartens or child-care centers are either teachers or appren-tice teachers. In France, to work in a *crèche maternelle* you need more qualifications than a public school teacher—additional courses in child development and public health. When I recently interviewed Michel Rocard, who served as French prime minis-ter from 1988 to 1991, he told me that his proudest success in resisting austerity demands was preventing the budget cutters from reducing the qualifications and pay of pre-kindergarten teachers.

But in America, how can we possibly make all human-service jobs into good jobs? Start with the fact that at least 60 percent of the funding for these jobs is ultimately public money. Government pays upward of half of all health-care costs through Medicare, Medicaid, the State Children's Health Insurance Program, the Veterans Administration, and the health insurance of public employees. The vast majority of nursing-home care is paid by Medicaid. Home care is heavily subsidized by public agencies. And in early-childhood education and day care, while the afflu-ent may have nannies or private day-care arrangements, Head Start is a public program and state, local, and federal agencies subsidize day care through a variety of social service programs.

Clearly, the government has the leverage to set standards. The federal Davis-Bacon Act is a rough model. It was enacted in 1931 to assure that non-union construction contractors would not undercut prevailing wage scales. Davis-Bacon requires that all federally funded construction pay prevailing wages, which in practice turns out to mean union-scale wages.

Davis-Bacon has its critics. There was a time when union bargaining power was accused of stimulating inflation by driving contract settlements that increased wages and benefits in excess of the rate of productivity growth. Whatever the reality of that ancient charge, that era is long gone. Today the problem is the opposite—wages lag far behind productivity increases, and the gains go instead to the top.

America needs a good-jobs strategy. And human-service jobs are a fine place to begin.

The new administration could require that any job in the human services supported in whole or in part by federal funds would have to pay a professional wage and be part of a career track. A minimum starting annual salary might be $24,000 a year, or about $12 an hour, which compares with hourly pay levels of $6 or $7 that are now common in nurse-aide, home-care, and child-care work. Opportunities for genuine advancement with pay increases would have to be part of the plan. Rather than using budget pressures to cut these wages, national policy would seek to raise them.

For example, instead of defining a nurse-aide as a high-turnover, low-qualification, low-pay occupation, the job would require substantially more training. Some of the training could be done on the job. With more training and qualifications, these workers could be entrusted with more responsibilities, and nursing-home residents would get better care. Such jobs would also be entry points to higher-level positions, such as licensed practical nurse.

In the area of pre-kindergarten and day care, all such jobs would be considered teaching jobs rather than the high-turnover, largely custodial jobs of the current system. Raising the qualifications and pay of pre-k teachers would be part of a national strategy of universal pre-kindergarten, on a level at least that of public school teachers.

Some have argued that you don't need much training to babysit kids or provide basic care to senescent old folks. In fact, the development of young children and the quality of life of the elderly are profoundly affected by the quality of their caregivers. One of the best-established findings of recent research on child development is that a dollar invested in early-childhood education is one of the most cost-effective investments we can make. The difference between child development and babysitting, of course, depends on the availability of well-trained professionals who work with young children. Likewise, in the care of the elderly, having well-trained people improves not just seniors' comfort but also their physical health, cognitive stimulation, and capacity to live fulfilling lives.

We have seen the beginning of a rough model of this kind of upgrading and professionalization in the strategies of unions that represent home-care workers. Home-care workers are often classified as independent contractors. As a result, they have no bargaining power, and public and nonprofit agencies often try to solve their own budget problems by paying home-care workers as little as possible. This creates a vicious circle of burnout and high turnover, even though the vast majority of these workers are conscientious and eager to perform well. Recently, in several states led by California, the SEIU and the American Federation of State County and Municipal Employees (AFSCME) have succeeded in persuading legislatures and governors to approve laws or executive orders establishing public agencies with which home-care workers can bargain collectively, as well as providing additional public funds. In Alameda County in California, the typical wage went from $4.25 to $10 an hour.

Another pressing need is public subsidy to help low-wage human-service workers ascend career ladders. In some occupations, these ladders exist in principle, and there are heartening individual stories of the nurse-aide who graduated to licensed practical nurse, or the classroom aide who went to night school and earned a teaching credential. Despite a few model programs, however, our society seems determined to make this path as arduous as possible. Almost by definition, someone working for $6 or $7 an hour, often with family responsibilities, has an extreme shortage of time as well as money. Though some rare individuals do succeed, it takes uncommon tenacity and self-sacrifice, and sometimes the sacrifice of one's own children. Why should we make this so hard? Other societies provide subsidies for living expenses during training.

This effort would be part of two broader labor policy shifts that America sorely needs. First, we need to reverse the trend toward casualization of labor that has been occurring for three decades. One of the great advances of the twentieth century was regularization of the employment relationship. Through successful social struggle, growth of unions, and enactment of legislation, most jobs came to provide decent wages and fringe benefits. Workers could not be fired without cause. Loyalty to the firm was reciprocated. Grievance systems were created and respected. Economists termed these jobs primary labor-market jobs. Casual, secondary labor-market jobs, which paid less and offered no such guarantees, continued to exist, but they were the exception. In recent years, however, the shift to casual jobs has become the norm, and in low-paid human-service work, casual, high-turnover jobs are the industry standard.

Second, the upgrading of human-service work would reverse another insidious trend: employers' habit of trying to increase the efficiency of labor by fragmenting jobs into separate tasks and paying the lowest possible wage for each task—a strategy known as Taylorism, after the early-twentieth-century "efficiency expert" Fredrick Winslow Taylor, who first recommended it.

However, when it comes to human services, many of the supposed gains of Taylorism are false economies. Studies of nursing homes have shown that better-trained and -paid workers can head off expensive conditions such as bedsores. Whereas registered nurses once performed a multiplicity of tasks and became very familiar with each patient, many hospitals have created a plethora of lower-wage occupations—phlebotomists to draw blood, technicians to perform tests, nurse-aides to take blood pressures—leaving the RN to cover more patients and do a far narrower range of tasks. But when the Massachusetts General Hospital ran an experiment, putting all care on one floor directly in the hands of RNs, the results were better patient outcomes and a more efficient use of human resources. The upgrading of human-service work would be part of an overdue process of reversing Taylorism. More workers would use a broader range of human skills to care for whole human beings.

As I suggested in chapter 1, an expansive good-jobs strategy on this scale would take a lot of money. A rough estimate of the cost of upgrading all low-wage human-service work into decent professional employment with career paths is about $150 billion a year. That includes the cost of providing universal, high-quality pre-kindergarten and child care, which is generally estimated at about $50 billion a year.

That's serious money, particularly if you are invoking conventional budget assumptions that predate the current recession and financial collapse—though it's not so much compared with the cost of military operations in Iraq and Afghanistan, now budgeted at $188 billion annually, or next to the $2.4 trillion ten-year cost of the Bush tax cuts, or the cost of economic collapse. To put this in perspective, $150 billion a year is approximately 1 percent of gross domestic product.

Voters will embrace serious public spending only if we think big. Token outlays neither kindle the imagination nor improve lives. The promise of millions of good service-sector jobs that can't be exported—providing superior care to our children, our parents, and ourselves—is an example of the kind of idea that could capture the national imagination and revive the necessary political support for serious public outlay. It touches a national nerve of anxiety about where the good jobs will be for our children—and who will take care of us as we age. Certainly, we need a decent-work strategy for the entire economy. But human services are one place where the federal government has direct leverage.

Education and Training—with a Difference

It is hard to pick up a policy paper on American competitiveness without reading that better education and training is the silver bullet to cure our multiple problems. In the usual account, wages have been lagging because skills are lagging. A more educated workforce will also help America compete more effectively against a global workforce that increasingly includes not just cheaper routine production workers but also skilled designers, programmers, and engineers. The standard argument adds the point that retraining is also the remedy for "protectionism." Presumably, if we "take care of the losers" from trade, by subsidizing or training them while they find other jobs, the air will go out of the political opposition to trade deals.

This account is misleading or incomplete in several respects. First, while we do need a better-educated workforce, education is only one of the determinants of worker wages. Another crucial influence is power. Union workers at, say, hotels organized by UNITE-HERE earn middle-class wages and fringe benefits—and enjoy opportunities to train for better jobs. The only difference between them and similar hotel workers who earn subsistence wages is the presence or absence of the union. There is a connection to training, but the cause-and-effect runs in the opposite direction from the one usually proposed: It's not that routine hotel workers who come in with superior education levels command better pay; rather, the fact that management must pay better wages makes the corporate owners more likely to invest in worker training and retention, to get their money's worth.

Second, wages and salaries have been lagging inflation precisely during a period when more young Americans are completing college. Tens of millions of college grads find themselves working in jobs that do not require a college degree. The writing on a bitter T-shirt reads: "I have a liberal arts degree. Will that be for here or to go?" Even if millions of college students abandoned literature and philosophy for math and science, that would not solve the problem.

One thing America utterly lacks is what other nations call an active labor-market policy. The idea is not just to cultivate a broadly educated population but to subsidize the customized training of workers for emergent technologies, as well as their living expenses so that they can afford to train—and to do so at a scale sufficient to make a difference. This strategy is combined with a national commitment that there shall be no bad jobs; and that every job shall pay a true living wage, with the productivity to justify it.

Last year, I conducted a study of the country that comes closest to realizing this strategy, the small, highly trade-dependent nation of Denmark. The Danes call their model "flexicurity"—great labor-market flexibility combined with superb worker security. If that sounds like an oxymoron, the rest of the Danish model defies the usual economic categories and manages to square other several circles. I published my findings in the March–April 2008 issue of *Foreign Affairs*, but here are the headlines.

On the one hand, the Danes are passionate free traders. They score well in the ratings constructed by pro-market organizations. The World Economic Forum Competitiveness Index ranks Denmark third, just behind the United States and Switzerland, and even the far-right Heritage Foundation ranks Denmark eleventh, giving it demerits only for the size of its public sector. Denmark's financial markets are clean and transparent, its barrier to imports minimal, its labor markets the most flexible in Europe, its multinational corporations dynamic and largely unmolested by industrial policies, and its unemployment rate of 2.8 percent the second lowest in the OECD.

On the other hand, Denmark spends about 50 percent of its

GDP socially and has the world's second-highest tax rate after Sweden, as well as strong trade unions and one of the world's most equal income distributions. For the half of GDP that they pay in taxes, the Danes get not just universal health insurance but also generous child-care and family-leave arrangements, unemployment compensation that typically covers around 95 percent of lost wages, free higher education, secure pensions in old age, and the world's most creative system of worker retraining.

What makes the flexicurity model both attractive to workers and dynamic for society are six key features: full employment; strong unions recognized as social partners; fairly equal wages among different sectors, so that a shift from manufacturing to service-sector work does not typically entail a pay cut; employer freedom to hire and fire as necessary; a comprehensive income floor; and a set of labor-market programs that spend an astonishing 4.5 percent of Danish GDP on programs such as transitional unemployment assistance, wage subsidies, and highly customized retraining. In return for such spending, the unions actively support both employer flexibility and a set of tough rules to weed out welfare chiselers; workers are understood to have duties as well as rights.

A Danish worker who becomes unemployed can collect generous benefits. However, the worker cannot just sit idle, but must take advantage of a wide range of educational and training opportunities, most of which will lead to a job as good as or better than the old one. This system is not cheap—but it produces the holy grail of economic and social policy: an economy that is highly dynamic and competitive as well as one without extremes of wealth and poverty.

For the United States, 4.5 percent of GDP would be about $600 billion a year. Current US spending on all forms of government labor-market subsidies—most of which consist of meager and strictly time-limited unemployment compensation—is about 0.3 percent of GDP, less than $50 billion. The dynamic US economy has plenty of flexibility but little security. Denmark suggests that a different path is possible.

The Danish model squares another circle by reconciling free trade with economic security. This is not an easy feat. In a global system, corporations can move around in search of low taxes, cheap labor, and scant social regulation. Yet in Denmark, even trade unionists are passionate free traders. Marina Hoffmann, chief economist of the Danish Metalworkers Federation, improbably told me, "We are a small country and we survive by exporting . . . If a Danish multinational manufacturing corporation can be more competitive by outsourcing components, we will be more competitive as a nation."

In other words, hiving off routine production jobs to China and Eastern Europe helps keep higher-end, knowledge-based design and engineering jobs in Denmark. And as manufacturing becomes more automated, a national policy of professionalizing service-sector jobs takes up much of the slack. A nursing-home worker in Denmark, for example, gets far more training, status, and pay than one in the United States.

In much of the rest of Europe, labor-market rigidities have been blamed for high unemployment rates and for a welfare state of "insiders and outsiders" in which the well employed fiercely protect their jobs at the expense of those with little or nothing. It is here that Denmark offers its most ingenious blend of free markets and social democracy: Despite heavy unionization, there are no regulations against laying off workers.

In fact, Denmark has Europe's highest rate of labor turnover, and much of it is voluntary. A 2005 Eurobarometer poll found that more than 70 percent of Danes think it a good thing to change jobs frequently, compared with fewer than 30 percent in neighboring Germany. Danish respondents reported that they had changed employers an average of six times, the highest figure in the European Union. One in three Danes changes jobs every year. And with employers free to deploy workers as they wish, and all Danes eligible for generous social benefits, there is no inferior "temp" industry, because there is no need for it. As precarious short-term contract employment has grown in most other countries, the number of Danes in temporary contracts has decreased since the mid-1980s. Where most other OECD nations have a knot of middle-aged people stuck in long-term unemployment, in Denmark the vast majority of the unemployed return to work within six months, and the number of long-term unemployed is vanishingly small.

Thanks to its active labor-market policies, Denmark has the world's highest percentage of workers, 47 percent, in some form of continuing education. The highly productive workforce helps both large and specialized Danish export industries thrive. Denmark is a global leader in such niche exports as hearing-aid production (through world-class companies such as Oticon), consumer electronics (Bang & Olufsen), insulin (Novo Nordisk), environmental technology, and finely engineered plumbing fixtures. As a seafaring nation, Denmark hosts global shipping giants such as Maersk, which ranks 138th on the Global Fortune 500 list. Wages in Denmark are about 70 percent above the OECD average, but the high productivity of the Danish work-force justifies them.

Denmark's flexicurity system did not spring full-grown from the brows of policy intellectuals. It is the fruit of more than a century of consensual social bargaining with the unions as full partners, punctuated by periodic crises. The current system dates to the early 1990s, a period when Denmark was suffering from stubbornly high unemployment. At the time, some prime-aged, able Danes were using unemployment and disability benefits to stay out of the labor force, often for life—an embarrassment to the work ethic that was rendering the system unaffordable and undermining its legitimacy.

In a typically Danish compromise, the unions agreed to support a crackdown on abuses by reducing eligibility for unemployment compensation from nine years to four and creating individual-ized reemployment plans that required the unemployed to meet regularly with their counselors to seek new jobs, often in new occupations. The labor movement's commitment, after all, is to facilitating and rewarding work, not idleness. This brand of tough love forced many of Denmark's unemployed to seek and find jobs, often without the help of the system's job centers. And in return, the Danish government increased resources for highly customized training and temporary wage subsidies.

An unemployed Dane who reports to a job center can qualify for such opportunities as adult apprenticeships and university-level education. Employer freedoms to lay off workers were also reaffirmed, helping to bring down unemployment. According to former finance minister Mogens Lykketoft, one of the key designers of the new strategy, "When companies are aware of the fact that it is possible to get rid of the manpower when market conditions change, they will not hesitate to hire new people at an upswing."

Despite the coincidence of timing and some superficially similar elements, the Danish reforms of the 1990s were not remotely like welfare reform in the United States. The Danish unemployment benefit for a median-income family of four can be 95 percent of the prior wage. In the United States, it is about 30 percent. Whereas Danes can draw benefits for four years, the typical US limit is six months. With the exception of small pilot programs, neither the US welfare system nor the US unemployment system offers sufficient support to enable people to cover living expenses while they are undergoing retraining. And in the United States, a shift from a manufacturing job to the service sector typically means a very significant pay cut.

What would an active labor-market policy look like for the United States? There are elements of it in some state retraining and wage-subsidy programs, and in federal job training programs. But the scale is too small to make a difference, and the training is seldom combined with a commitment to increase wages. A serious policy would combine good jobs with the necessary job training, and subsidize living expenses while people trained. But we are nowhere near such a comprehensive program.

One trendy idea promoted by center-right American economists is wage insurance. The idea is to compel displaced workers to take a job, any job, and the government would pay half the difference between the old job and the new one for a limited period, say three years. For example, a laid-off steelworker who had been earning $21 an hour would take a job at Wal-Mart for $7. For three years, the government would pay half the difference—$7—leaving the worker with $14 or a 33-percent cut. After three years, the worker would have only the $7 wage, a 66-percent cut.

Another ineffectual compromise is Trade Adjustment Assistance. The idea is to channel similar transitional assistance as well as retraining aid to workers who can prove that they have been displaced by trade. But huge sums get wasted deliberating over whether trade caused a particular job loss. And as economist Alan Blinder, former vice chairman of the Federal Reserve, has written, for every job directly affected by the pressures of low-wage global competition, many others suffer reduced wages.

The genius of the Danish model is that it's for everyone. It is part of a far broader national commitment to a highly egalitarian society where there are no bad jobs and to the use of ongoing labor-market subsidies to create a highly skilled and dynamic workforce as the essence of global competitiveness. If a US administration had the political nerve to propose active labor-market policies at a serious scale, it could do more than just narrow income gaps and increase overall productivity: It might also reclaim some of the lost support for a more managed brand of capitalism, revive the idea of a role for government in promoting efficiency as well as equality, reclaim trade unions as social partners, and build more compassion among Americans of different social strata.

An Apollo-Scale Commitment to Renewable Energy

The energy and climate crisis links three of America's most pressing problems: national security, the environment, and the economy. As Al Gore recently put it, "We're borrowing money from China to buy oil from the Persian Gulf to burn it in ways that destroy the planet. Every bit of that's got to change." The cost of imported oil, now running at $2 billion a day, equals nearly our entire trade imbalance. In other words, if we shifted entirely to renewable energy, we would have virtually no trade deficit and far less imported inflation.

The cure for the energy crisis and the related catastrophe of global climate change can also be a big part of our strategy for economic recovery. The measures that would drastically cut our carbon emissions would also create millions of well-paying new domestic jobs and new clean industries. Some of the jobs would be directly related to advanced technologies—jobs in research and development, engineering, and manufacturing. Others would be new variations on more traditional jobs—construction work installing advanced solar panels rather than conventional roofs, or building and rebuilding houses to make them more energy-efficient. But virtually all of these jobs would pay middle-class wages or better.

A national clean-energy policy would also be a salutary ideological reversal, for it would require us to resurrect the virtuous practice of economic planning. "Planning" implies bureaucracy, but every time government enacts a tax credit or contracts for a technology, it is a form of unacknowledged planning. Often, planning facilitates markets. Planning and devoting serious public investment for sustainable energy would be yet another teachable moment in the necessary and beneficial potential of government. The idea of government planning has been widely ridiculed by conservative economists for more than a generation. How could government dare to think that it could "pick winners"? How could government possibly know more than markets?

As it happens, the genius of free markets is rather tarnished right now. And the current crises of energy and environment, along with the financial collapse, suggest that only government can divert us from our present disastrous course.

As Sir Nicholas Stern said in his now famous report on the costs of doing nothing, global climate change is history's greatest case of market failure. Markets systematically priced pollution too cheaply. Market mechanisms systematically underinvested in clean, renewable energy technologies and overinvested in dirty ones. Government intervention is necessary to turn us to a more efficient and sustainable path that markets are too myopic to discern.

History shows how government planning aimed at a widely shared national goal can create entire new industries. In the World War I era, government subsidized and organized the post-Wright-brothers generation of aviation technology as well as the civil aviation industry. Government planning turned radio from a curiosity into a military necessity and then a mass consumer good. The Radio Corporation of America (RCA) was a government invention. We are still living off the spillover benefits of World War II—everything from jet aviation to the beginnings of advanced computing. The Cold War and DARPA produced the early model of the Internet. The government subsidy of our great research universities, coupled with the work of the National Science Foundation and the National Institutes of Health, has made America a leader in biotechnology. In these and kindred enterprises, government does not "pick" winners. Government helps to *create* entirely new technological paths.

To reflect on all the industries whose course government has changed for the better is to appreciate how little the US government has done to change the trajectory of our energy policy. This passivity reflects the political influence of extractive industries—oil, gas, and coal—as well as our ideological antipathy to large-scale government planning. Of course, the $14 billion annual government subsidy to the oil industry, through tax breaks and royalty waivers, is a form of planning—it's just planning that reinforces the present path.

Government helps to develop new technologies that are beyond the ken of private supply and demand in four complementary ways. It can alter pricing and industrial and consumer behavior by regulation or by taxation. It can subsidize supply, and it can subsidize demand.

In the past, public policy has taken baby steps in all of these directions. The fuel-efficiency standards for automobiles that automakers fiercely resisted have modestly improved mileage—and along the way stimulated technical progress. The 1990 acid rain amendments to the Clean Air Act set overall limits on sulfur dioxide emissions, and then used a marketlike mechanism of tradable emission permits to achieve them. But this "market" was entirely the creation of government policy overriding what private markets would otherwise have done.

Because of the default of federal leadership, a great deal of progress on the renewable-energy and clean-environment fronts has come from states, localities, and citizens. Their success has been limited because of the absence of complementary national policies. But environmental progress has been a model of bottom-up innovation and citizen engagement. As the federal government takes on a leadership role, the decentralized and democratic aspect of the planning process should be honored and deepened, not supplanted by federal bureaucrats. The cure for bureaucracy is not always the market; often it is citizenship.

The federal government has very modestly subsidized the creation of cleaner technologies such as solar and wind (along with massive subsidies to the nuclear power industry). Federal, state, and local governments have also subsidized or regulated demand. For example, states have tried to accelerate the development and use of solar and wind technology by requiring that utilities purchase a certain proportion of their energy from renewable sources by a certain year. The hope is that solar producers, assured of an expanding market, will then increase their investment and production capacity.

The point is that all of this needs to be taken to serious scale, and this can only be done via public investment, public regulation, and a reversal of current tax policies. Most energy is consumed in three venues: buildings, vehicles, and factories. There are great opportunities both for conservation and for new technologies in all three. All have the potential to increase domestic economic activity, restore technological leadership, and increase the supply of good jobs.

As Amory Lovins has been arguing for more than three decades, the most cost-effective way to reduce energy consumption is conservation. Many conservation measures have the virtue of being very labor-intensive, and most jobs insulating or retrofitting buildings pay well above minimum wage. New housing-development strategies to reward density and a new generation of energy-efficient mass transit can also be part of the mix, as can regulatory, tax, and subsidy measures to move more Americans into far-less-polluting cars.

For the foreseeable future, most Americans will be reliant on automobiles for much of their transportation. But they could be using cars that get a hundred miles per gallon rather than twenty or twenty-five, and in another generation they could be driving hydrogen-fuel-cell vehicles. People are already beginning to drive plug-in electric cars that do not consume petroleum-based fuels at all. Europe manages to use about half the energy relative to its GDP as the United States does. It achieves this not through a single silver bullet but via a very different mix of tax and subsidy policies that make mass transit cheaper and driving more expensive, as well as promoting conservation and an accelerated shift to renewable forms of energy.

There may be a strong moral case for a carbon tax as the most direct way to raise the price of oil, coal, and natural gas, thereby reducing carbon emissions directly. Other nations have much higher taxes on motor fuels. But at time when the American consumer has just been hit with a doubling in the retail price of gasoline, mandating more fuel-efficient cars and lowering the cost of nonpolluting forms of energy is probably a more viable strategy politically than raising the price of gas at the pump even higher. The tragedy is that the latest hike in the price of imported oil functions just like a tax. If we had added a $1-a-gallon tax back when the retail price of regular was $2, that revenue would be going into America's coffers—to subsidize development of domestic renewable energy—rather than into OPEC's.

The promise of more reliable energy through new technology appeals to America's can-do spirit. President Kennedy announced a commitment in 1961 to put a man on the moon by the end of the decade, and the subsequent Project Apollo ultimately cost about $70 billion a year as measured in current 2008 dollars. The Apollo Alliance for Renewable Energy has proposed a commitment of $30 billion a year for ten years. Its ten-point plan, released in its 2004 report *New Energy for America*, proposed to use a mix of tax credits, public subsidies, and investment to create 3.3 million new high-wage jobs in manufacturing, construction, transportation, high tech, and the public sector, while reducing dependence on foreign oil and cleaning up the environment.

In addition to the more than 3 million new jobs, Apollo's sponsors projected that its ten-year investment program would add $1.4 trillion to gross domestic product; add $953 billion in personal income and $323.9 billion in retail sales; and produce $284 billion in net energy-cost savings. Today, with oil trading at well above $100 a barrel and prices likely to keep rising, that energy savings would be closer to $1 trillion.

At the time of the 2004 Apollo report, $30 billion a year seemed a huge sum. But that was before the current economic crisis, the latest scientific findings about accelerating global climate change, the recent spike in the price of oil, and the most recent tallies of the cost of the Iraq War (close to $2 trillion). By now, $30 billion a year is probably too low.

US research and development in renewable energy, in both the public and private sectors, has actually fallen. According to testimony by Daniel Kammen, director of the Renewable and Appropriate Energy Laboratory at the University of California–Berkeley, investment in energy research is now $1 billion a year less than it was in the late 1990s. Research and development to incubate technologies that have not yet reached commercial maturity is one of the classic ways that government overcomes market failures. Current US research policy is the opposite of that in Japan, where government has worked closely with industry to lower the cost of new renewable forms of energy. According to Professor Kammen, a world-class R&D program led by the Japanese government produced a reduction of 8 percent per year for a decade in the cost of installed solar photovoltaic systems.

A comprehensive effort to move America to clean, renewable energy should be at the heart of a program of infrastructure renewal. Because of energy deregulation, our electricity grid is an archaic menace. Brownouts are frequent, and available energy-saving technologies such as "smart-metering"—which allows peak pricing and powering down—are largely absent. American business loses an estimated $120 billion a year due to power failures resulting from an inadequate grid. In many localities such as New York City, water and sewer systems are archaic time bombs. They leak like sieves, waste precious water, and fail to pursue opportunities to turn waste into energy.

In his most recent major speech, delivered on July 18, Al Gore proposed a very straightforward national goal. America's production of electricity should be based 100 percent on renewables within ten years. As Gore pointed out, enough sun falls on the surface of the earth every forty minutes to meet the planet's entire energy needs for a year. When demand increases, new technologies accelerate and costs fall. Gore reported, "The price of the specialized silicon used to make solar cells was recently as high as $300 per kilogram. But the newest contracts have prices as low as $50 a kilogram."

This is the kind of a national initiative that a leader as bold as Barack Obama could embrace and lead America to pursue. He has already embraced this change of policy direction rhetorically. The only thing that stands in the way is the premise that America cannot afford it. Under the Bush administration, America has been the world's leading obstacle to progress in reducing carbon emissions through the Kyoto process. Obama has already made clear that he would reverse that stance. But America also needs to become a leader in both its own conservation and conversion to renewables.

Obviously, there are many aspects of energy and environment policy beyond the scope of this brief book. In warning about the economic crisis that confronts the next president, I have chosen to emphasize sound environmental policies that are also good economic-recovery policies. For the long term, the road to an environmentally sustainable economy will require a great deal more.

Obama is moving in the right direction. His energy proposals, released August 4, announced a goal of getting "one million 150-mile-per-gallon plug-in hybrids on our roads within six years," as well as government subsidies to encourage their development and purchase. Obama called for a windfall-profits tax on oil companies, with the proceeds used to give families a $1,000 tax credit to partly compensate for rising fuel bills. The campaign's news release added: "Obama's emergency rebate plan is designed to help struggling families today while laying the groundwork for his long-term energy plan, which invests $150 billion per year [sic] in developing renewable technologies, encouraging energy efficiency and catalyzing the next generation of clean vehicles to end our dependence on foreign oil and create up to 5 million new jobs."

The reference to $150 billion *per year* in the press release was a typo. Obama's program actually calls for $150 billion over ten years, or just $15 billion a year. But to get serious about solving the problem, $150 billion a year would be more like it.

Universal Health Insurance: A Second Opinion

Many observers have assumed that Obama would make health reform one of his first and highest-profile initiatives. That, in my view, would be a mistake.

Unlike the financial collapse and the deepening recession, the fragility of reliable health insurance coverage was a big issue in 1993, when Bill Clinton failed to get health reform, and here we are fifteen years later with higher out-of-pocket costs and even less reliable coverage, and it is still a huge issue. But health reform will be one of most politically difficult of all of Obama's challenges. He may only get one shot at it. He should take a little more time until he has the stature to prevail and the plan to get reform right. It would be an a huge risk to spend large amounts of political capital and to stake the prestige of his entire presidency on health reform at the outset, as Bill Clinton disastrously did.

Obama has put forth a fairly modest version of incremental health reform. His plan would try to achieve close to universal coverage by building on the present system. Americans who had insurance and liked it could keep it. For those who could not afford insurance, there would be government subsidies. There would also be a "Medicare-like" public program, which individuals under age sixty-five, or employers, could buy into. Employers who failed to provide decent insurance would have to pay a tax. Obama hopes that costs would be contained both by greater and more transparent competition among plans and by increasing emphasis on public health and other wellness initiatives. He would also permit the importation of prescription drugs, and would rely on new computerized record keeping to achieve other cost savings.

Some critics have faulted Obama's plan for not making purchase of coverage mandatory. But that is the least of its deficiencies. The debate about whether health insurance should be a "mandate" is a classic example of the tendency of policy specialists to have tin political ears. In the economics classroom, a mandate is a neutral, technical term. In the political arena, the term suggests government coercion rather than government help. There is an immense ideological difference between offering subsidies and requiring citizens to go out and buy private insurance—and making insurance universal and automatic. Social Security is compulsory, tax-supported, and widely valued. Roosevelt was far too shrewd to call it a "mandate."

The main problem with Obama's current approach is that his plan builds on, and further complicates, a patchwork profit-driven system that is inherently inefficient. As we saw in chapter 3, many economists view escalating cost as the system's most serious problem. By expanding coverage without addressing the fundamental drivers of escalating cost, Obama (or his successor) risks a draconian cut in services later on.

According to the Centers for Medicare and Medicaid Services, total health outlays exceed $2.1 trillion a year, or better than $7,000 for every American man, woman, and child. Total health-care spending, now 16 percent of GDP, is projected to reach 20 percent in just seven years. The seemingly relentless medical inflation is widely attributed to many factors—the aging population; the proliferation of new technologies; poor diet and exercise; the tendency of supply (of physicians, hospitals, tests, pharmaceuticals, medical devices, and novel treatments) to generate its own demand; excessive litigation and defensive medicine; and tax-favored insurance coverage.

Demographics and medical technologies pose a cost challenge for every system—but ours is the outlier. European nations manage to cover everyone for less than 10 percent of GDP, and have better health outcomes. America's extreme failure to contain medical costs is primarily the result of our unique, pervasive commercialization. The dominance of for-profit insurance and pharmaceutical companies, a new wave of investor-owned specialty hospitals, and the defensive response by even nonprofit providers all raise costs and distort resource allocation. Profits, billing, and marketing costs siphon off $400 to $500 billion out of $2.1 trillion, but the more serious and less appreciated syndrome is the set of perverse incentives produced by commercial dominance.

Markets are said to optimize efficiencies. But despite a widespread view that competition is the key to cost containment, embraced by Obama and his health policy advisers, medicine—with its third-party payers and its partly social mission—does not lend itself to market discipline. Why not?

The private insurance system's main techniques for holding down costs are risk-selecting healthy patients, limiting services that will be covered, constraining payments to doctors and hospitals, and shifting costs to patients through rising deductibles and co-pays. But given the system's fragmentation and perverse incentives, much cost-effective care is squeezed out; resources are increasingly allocated in response to profit opportunities rather than medical need; many attainable efficiencies are not achieved; unnecessary medical interventions are made as long as they are profitable; administrative expenses are high; and enormous sums are squandered by various players seeking to game the system. The result is a perverse blend of overtreatment and undertreatment—and escalating cost. Reputable researchers calculate that between one-fifth and one-third of medical outlays do nothing to improve health.

Great improvements to health can be achieved by basic public health measures and a so-called population-based approach to wellness and medical care. But profit-maximizing entrepreneurs do not prosper by providing these services, and those who need them most are least likely to have insurance.

Innumerable studies have reported that consistent application of well-established standard protocols for such conditions as diabetes, asthma, and elevated cholesterol; screening for certain cancers; childhood immunizations; and diet and exercise can improve health and prevent costly treatment outlays later on. Comprehensive universal systems are far better equipped to realize these efficiencies, because everyone is covered and there are no incentives to pursue the most profitable patients or treatments rather than the ones dictated by medical need. Although most OECD countries have older populations than the United States, they have been far more effective at constraining costs without compromising care.

Many US insurers reward physicians for following standard clinical practices, but these incentives do not aggregate to an efficient national system of care. Commercial incentives are not fixing what's broken. Rather, cost-containment efforts fall heavily on the most heralded (and most abused) part of the system—the primary-care physician.

As insurance companies have attempted to constrain costs, primary-care doctors have seen caseloads rise, payments stagnate or decline, and allowable time per consultation dwindle. A popular strategy among cost-containment consultants is called income targeting. The idea is that physicians have a mental picture of expected earnings—an income target. If the insurance plan squeezes their income by reducing payments per visit, doctors will compensate by increasing their caseload and spending less time with each patient.

This false economy is a telling example of the myopia of commercialized managed care. A squeeze on primary doctors may indeed save the plan money in the short run, but as any practicing physician can testify, the strategy has multiple perverse effects. A doctor's most precious commodity is time—adequate time to review a chart, take a history, truly listen to a patient. You can't do all this in ten minutes. Harried primary-care doctors are more likely to miss cues, make mistakes, and—ironically enough—order more tests to cover their own lack of time for hands-on assessment, as well as making more referrals to expensive specialists for procedures that the primary-care doctor could perform more cost-effectively given adequate time and compensation. But the gap between generalist and specialist pay is widening.

A second commercial cost-containment device is the use of increased deductibles and co-pays. The frank purpose is to dissuade people from going to the doctor. But sometimes seeing the doctor is medically indicated, and waiting until conditions are dire costs the system far more money than it saves. Moreover, the 85 million Americans who have periods of noncoverage during some point every year are even less likely to seek preventive care.

Yet another perversely inflationary aspect of the present system is its effect on the revenue-maximization strategies of hospitals. Large hospitals, which still have substantial bargaining power with insurers, necessarily cross-subsidize services. The ER may lose money, but cardiology makes a bundle. So hospitals fiercely

defend their profit centers. They invest heavily, often duplica-
tively, in facilities to attract physicians and patients for lucrative
procedures. For the system as a whole, it would be far more cost-
effective to shift resources from subspecialists to primary care. But
in a fragmented, commercial system the specialists might take
their business elsewhere, so they have the leverage to maintain
incomes and privileges. In principle, insurers inject discipline.
But in practice, the endless cat-and-mouse game between payers
and providers only yields new ways to maximize profits—and
seldom by achieving the optimal match of need and care.

A comprehensive national system is far better positioned to
match resources with needs—and not by "rationing" care. Our
system has the most de facto rationing—high rates of noncoverage, preexisting condition exclusions, excessive deductibles and
co-pays, shorter hospital stays, and rushed physician visits. A
universal system suffers far less of the feast-or-famine misalloca-
tion of resources driven by profit maximization. It also saves huge
sums that our system wastes on administration, billing, marketing, profit, executive compensation, and risk selection. When the
British National Health Service faced a shortage of primary-care
doctors, it adjusted pay schedules and the shortage diminished.
Our commercialized system is evidently incapable of producing
that result.

As we saw in chapter 3, the assumption that a single comprehensive system is politically out of the question puts America
on a path that would combine nominal universal coverage with
deterioration in what is actually covered, plus acceleration of
cost-shifting to individuals. We are becoming a nation that is
underinsured, even though health economists fret about insurance coverage that is overly generous. Over time, we are moving
inexorably toward a system in which only the affluent who can
pay out of pocket get the care that they need. This is all a consequence of relying on fragmented private insurance.

I have long argued that there are fundamentally different kinds
of incremental reform. One merely bloats existing, inefficient

systems and locks them in, making transformational change more difficult. The other sneaks up on radical change. For example, Barack Obama has included as part of his proposed health reform universal coverage of children. But he would achieve that goal by building on the existing system of patchwork public and private programs. It would be far better to give very child a Medicare card. Kids are the cheapest group of people to insure. They seldom get seriously ill, and with children investments in wellness and prevention pay off handsomely. If every child had Medicare, we would demonstrate to American families the efficiency and convenience of a single universal system. And we would be building a rolling constituency for making Medicare truly universal—for prime-aged adults as well as the old and the young.

Thus my advice to Obama on the health reform front: Get your sea legs, address more pressing crises, demonstrate inspirational leadership—and take a little more time to get this right.

Trade and Globalization

Every recent Democratic president and most major Democratic candidates have been tripped up by the issue of trade policy. Senior Democrats listen to economists and business elites who counsel them that only fools and toadies for special interests oppose something called "free trade" (which is really an artificial construct). These same financial elites promote deals like NAFTA, which is less about trade and more about access to investment opportunities, often on terms that disadvantage smaller nations dependent on the goodwill and the export markets of the United States. These same politicians also hear from workers and trade unionists and community leaders who are harmed by the outsourcing of jobs and the battering down of wages produced by cheaper foreign wage competition.

More often than not, candidates split the difference. They

disclaim and denounce an equally misleading straw man known as "protectionism," but hasten to add that they are for "fair trade." They also criticize nations that subsidize exports, manipulate currencies, and discriminate against products made in the United States; and invariably they call for labor and environmental provisions in trade deals as well as fairer currency alignments. Then they change the subject as rapidly as possible.

Here is Obama on trade, speaking in April to the Alliance for American Manufacturing:

> The truth is, trade is here to stay. We live in a global economy. For America's future to be as bright as our past, we have to compete. We have to win.
>
> Not every job that has left is coming back. And not every job lost is due to trade—automation has made plants more efficient so they can make the same amount of steel with few workers. These are the realities.
>
> I also don't oppose all trade deals. I voted for two of them because they have the worker and environmental agreements I believe in. Some of you disagreed with me on this but I did what I thought was right.
>
> That's the truth. But let me tell you what else I believe in. For America to win, American workers have to win, too . . . That's why I opposed NAFTA, it's why I opposed CAFTA, and it's why I said any trade agreement I would support had to contain real, enforceable standards for workers.
>
> That's why I believe the Permanent Normalized Trade agreement with China didn't do enough to ensure fairness and compliance.

Obama went on to spell out a much tougher trade line with China, as well as subsidies to rebuild the US manufacturing base. The speech was better, and more detailed, than most. But still more is required, both in public policy and in public education.

The debate about "free trade" versus "protectionism" is a false one. The fact is that all trade depends on rules. The real question is: Whom do the rules benefit? And which rules might be more symmetrical?

There's no such thing as totally free trade. Business depends on enforcement of its property rights, its ability to have its assets overseas protected from confiscation, the honoring of its patents and trademarks, its right to collect profits from foreign operations and bring them home, and protections against other unfair trade practices. Business welcomes these government intrusions.

So it's pointless to look for some kind of holy grail of pure free trade, because it doesn't exist. What we need is a balance of benefits—for ourselves and our trading partners; and for business, workers, and consumers—just as we seek a balanced economy at home.

When progressives began their efforts to balance predatory capitalism with social rights more than a century ago, property rights were paramount and other rights did not exist. As Americans and Europeans invented the modern mixed economy, citizenship rights balanced the rights of capital. Social insurance eased hardship, and taxes were raised to pay for programs of retirement and health security. The absolute license of employers was constrained, with regulations on wages, hours, working conditions, and workplace safety. The state guaranteed the right of workers to organize. Financial regulations limited the tendency of capital markets to produce cycles of boom and bust. A little later came environmental standards and other consumer protections, all of which put necessary social constraints on how business could operate. Entrepreneurs still thrived—certain low roads were just off limits.

Today business elites would like to return to the world of 1880—all property rights and no offsetting social rights. And globalization makes that goal easier, because it allows business to move to locations with weak taxes, regulations, and labor protections. That in turn puts pressure on nations with decent citizen and worker protections to lower their own standards—as the US and EU nations have lately lowered taxes on capital, in turn making ordinary citizens pay more to finance social benefits.

So the issue is not really "trade," as ordinarily used in debates about in trade agreements. The real question is *how to govern capitalism* now that capitalism is global. It is akin to questions that Americans have been debating in domestic policy for more than a century. But domestically, the government is sovereign. Globally, public authority is weak and divided. Obama would do an immense service to the clarity of public debate and to the array of policy choices now beyond respectable discussion if he could reframe the issue on those terms.

There has been a great deal of nonsense in these debates about how, in an electronic age, the genie is out of the bottle and there is no way to constrain global capital for the public good. In fact, global investment flows traveled at the speed of light in 1930, and even in 1890. They just flowed over telegraph wires rather than the Internet. And after the Great Depression, governments then in power acted in concert to limit speculative global flows of capital. Today, as reflection of a dramatic shift in political power back to big business, we have a system of global rules biased against social and economic regulation. We could have very different rules.

In many respects, the damage caused by speculative global capital is a more serious threat to a socially balanced economy than are the dislocations caused by trade with low-wage countries. In my travels to Denmark, I found that the highly productive Danes could coexist, at least for now, with low-wage imports from Asia. What was menacing their social bargain were private equity funds looking for quick returns that had no respect for Danish workers or the Danish collaborative model.

The challenge is complicated by the emergence of nations such as China that are nominally communist and that use the economic and political power of the state to violate the ordinary rules of markets, as well as the rights of citizens. Yet American and other multinational corporations are delighted to work with the Chinese dictatorship because it provides well-trained, intimidated, and docile workers. The People's Republic also sometimes provides immense subsidies to lure advanced US production abroad, at the expense of the American economy.

Other Asian nations such as Japan and Korea are democracies, but they don't share conservative American conceptions of free markets. They also use tight alliances between the state and large corporations both to create and to capture competitive advantage. Yet an administration that is very aggressive when it comes to defending what it takes to be America's military security is remarkably feeble when it comes to defending our global economic security. The clearest explanation is that the administration's constituents in the nation's boardrooms can make huge profits wherever production is located, and have ceased identifying their own economic interests with those of the country.

John Kerry, the Democrats' 2004 nominee, delivered a nice applause line when he spoke of "Benedict Arnold CEOs," but he did not have a coherent policy to match (and his fundraisers directed him to stop using the line, which was offending his donors). Clinton largely carried out the business agenda of globalization, tempered by only the most modest gestures on labor standards.

Obama's historic task is to reframe the entire conversation and point us toward a new system of global rules that create better balance both in the permissible practices of trading nations and in the relative protections for property, for labor, and for the environment. Side agreements are not enough. And as we have seen from the examples elsewhere in this chapter of Danish-style labor-market policies, stronger unions, public works, strategies to professionalize human-service work, and universal health insurance, much of what we need to do to counteract the negative effects of globalization begins at home.

Re-regulating capitalism on a global scale is a systemic challenge on a par with solving global warming. And the two challenges are directly connected. As James Gustave Speth, one of the most eminent environmentalists of our times, writes in his new book *The Bridge at the Edge of the World,* the systemic failure to address climate change is first and foremost a failure of capitalism as presently structured. Bringing standards of labor, environmental, and financial regulation to a global scale will all be required. Raising labor and living standards in the third world will help workers in poor nations realize more of the fruits of their own hard work and rising productivity, even as it prevents a global race to the bottom. This also requires substantial revision of prevailing ideology and language—something only a president can do.

Costs and Benefits

As I suggested in chapter 1, a recovery program on this scale will not be cheap. But the alternative is for America to risk prolonged financial crisis and remain on a path of increasing economic insecurity. What would it cost? In the first year, emergency public works and financial recapitalization could easily cost $300 billion each. That's about $600 billion, or about 4 percent of GDP. That money, as noted in chapter 1, is available from a combination of repealing Bush's tax cuts, increasing tax enforcement on the shelters used by the very wealthy, winding down the war, and a modest temporary increase in deficit spending.

By early 2010, most of the costs of onetime emergency bailouts would be behind us, and the rest of the program would begin kicking in. The annual increased costs would be at the following order of magnitude:

Permanent investment in public infrastructure:	200 billion
Energy independence	100 billion
Active labor-market policy	100 billion
Restoration of other social-outlay and intergovernmental aid	100 billion

Professionalization of human-service work	100 billion
Universal pre-kindergarten and better day care	50 billion
Housing subsidies	50 billion
Savings from military cuts	-100 billion
Total net increase:	**600 billion**

Six hundred billion dollars is, again, about 4 percentage points of our GDP. It would increase total federal spending from its current level of about 20 percent of GDP in 2007 to about 24 percent of GDP. The previous peak, in 1983, was 23.5 percent. So this shift is not exactly revolutionary fiscally—but the impact on the lives of Americans would be transformational.

I have made no assumptions about the increased federal revenues resulting from enhanced economic activity and workers with higher incomes contributing more in tax revenues. But there would surely be some positive offset. The net additional cost could well be 3 percent of GDP or less.

I have left universal health insurance out of this chart, because offsetting benefits would leave the medium-term cost neutral at worst. For example, according to the economist Dean Baker, we could eliminate the infamous doughnut hole in Bush's prescription drug coverage simply by getting rid of insurance industry middlemen and putting the program under public Medicare. According to calculations by the blue-chip Lewin Group, a universal health insurance program such as the Hacker plan would increase public outlays in the first year by about $50 billion—but would produce a ten-year economic savings of $1 trillion.

This general program is more expansive than much of what Obama has proposed. It would require a transformation in public and elite opinion, and in some cases of Obama's own preconceptions. But the seeds of this approach can be found in his core values and speeches. And nothing less will return the economy to a path of broad prosperity.

| five |

A Work in Progress

One day you finally knew
What you had to do
Though the voices around you
Kept shouting
Their bad advice . . .

. . . But little by little
As you left their voices behind
The stars began to burn
Through the sheets of clouds
And there was a new voice
Which you slowly
Recognized as your own

> —MARY OLIVER, "THE JOURNEY"

Barack Obama has rare skills of leadership, and he will take office amid a deepening crisis that will sorely test him and the American people. At the end of chapter 3, I stitched together from several of Obama's addresses and writings a compelling speech that sounded like the words of another Franklin Roosevelt. With less representative but still accurate selections, I might have assembled one that made Obama sound pretty tame. As we have seen from the campaign, Obama is a work in progress. But I am betting that he possesses both the character and the political nerve to rise to the occasion—as well as the occasion to rise to.

The argument of this book invites several different kinds of skepticism. Some would say that the proposed program is not wise policy; or that the crisis is not really that severe; or that it couldn't possibly win enactment; or that Obama, like the early Roosevelt, is a chameleon. And wouldn't it make more sense if Obama just governed as a moderate liberal, or tried to build bipartisan consensus from the political center, as so many commentators have urged, after the divisive, radical conservatism of George W. Bush?

Many observers, who have noted his appeal to conservatives as well as liberals, see Obama as a post-partisan bridge builder. It was this aspect of his now famous Red State/Blue State/United States convention address in 2004 that struck such a powerful chord.

The sociologist and commentator Amitai Etzioni, for instance, has written of Obama's attraction as a "communitarian"—a rather loosely defined ideology that incorporates some conservative as well as liberal elements. One can discern that appeal in Obama's embrace of religious values, his powerful speeches on the importance of black fathers, and his strong sense of family and of the mutual obligation in the American family. Etzioni adds, "A revival of the American community requires us to spend much less of our energy and resources on fighting one another, and invest much more of it in the common good, in those goods that serve one and all. Hence, Obama seeks not only social justice for the poor, but decent work at decent wages for one and all; he harps less on the uninsured, and seeks a health care system that will encompass all Americans . . ." (If that is "communitarian," fine with me. It sounds pretty much like effective liberalism.)

Several prominent conservative Republicans have likewise warmed to Obama, partly because of their revulsion at the perversion of conservatism under Bush—the fiscal excesses, the corruption and incompetence in running government, the assault on liberties, and the assertion of overweening executive power. Obama supporter Bruce Bartlett, a well-known conservative economist and commentator who served in the Reagan and Bush I administrations, wrote an influential piece in *The*

New Republic last June listing all the conservative notables who are supporting Obama—and not just because of Bush-fatigue. Bartlett quotes Christine Allison, wife of a former president of the late William F. Buckley's *National Review,* and a woman who has never before voted for a Democrat. "He speaks with candor and elegance against the kind of politics that have become so dispiriting and for the kind of America I would like to see," she wrote in *The Dallas Morning News.* "I find Mr. Obama to be prudent, thoughtful, and courageous. His life story embodies the conservative values that go to the core of my beliefs."

One of Obama's broad appeals to conservatives as well as liberals is that his personal life is one of probity and decency, as well of diligent accomplishment. One contributing cause of the broad disaffection from politics in recent years is what might be called the Yuck factor—adolescent moral lapses that infected senior figures in both parties. (He did *what?* Yuck!)

In this rogues' gallery, Obama's worst sin is that he sneaks an occasional cigarette. He has an irreproachable private life. When he joined a weekly poker game in Springfield, Illinois, mainly to get to know other legislators socially, he let it be known that a bimbo who accompanied another (married) legislator was not welcome. Attending a meeting of the Congressional Black Caucus's annual retreat, he was disgusted by the wide availability of prostitutes. There is a narrow line between probity and prudery, but one of his undeniable appeals to conservatives—and to women—is that Obama is an upstanding family man.

Finding no other character flaw in him, the McCain campaign rather lamely tried lampooning Obama as "The One"—arrogant, vain, self-important, elitist. What an act of sheer gall to paint an African American from humble origins who made his way through college and law school on scholarships as "elitist." The Republicans stopped just short of using the word *uppity.* It came off more as sour grapes.

Community, Government, and Self-Reliance

But wouldn't an expansive use of government spending and regulation undercut Obama's cross-party appeal? Not if it is done right. After all, the Reverend Martin Luther King Jr. based his campaign for redemption of civil rights on deeply held religious faith, but also called for a dramatic expansion of federal outlay for economic as well as racial justice. Programs such as increased support for working families can help parents do better by their children. There is hardly a conflict between economic recovery and strong community. Conservatives used to say that the best antidote to poverty is a job—and they are right—but the job needs to pay a living wage.

One of the great conservative myths of recent years is the idea that affirmative government and individual initiative are somehow at odds. Tell that to a person from a lower-income family who worked part-time to attend one of our great state universities or public community colleges; or a diligent worker who suffered a disabling injury and was saved from destitution by Social Security disability checks and federally mandated workers' compensation, then was re-employed thanks to the rights guaranteed by the Americans with Disabilities Act; or a family with a desperately ill child who was able to get the necessary treatment from Medicaid; or a scientist who spent long hours making a breakthrough discovery thanks to an NSF or NIH grant. That tradition needs to be reclaimed and strengthened. Obama has repeatedly debunked the conservative "Ownership Society" as one in which government leaves you on your own.

Before Bill Clinton's compelling rhetoric was undermined by budget-balance fever, he effectively managed to connect broadly shared traditional values of personal initiative with liberal forms of help. His phrase from the 1992 campaign, "People who work hard and play by the rules shouldn't be poor," perfectly captured both sides of the equation. Most Americans indeed think people should work hard and not chisel. And most Americans also think that a job should be sufficient to keep workers out of poverty. Only effective government policy can deliver on the latter promise.

Unlike Clinton, who faced severe ideological headwinds of antipathy to government, Obama takes office at a moment when the previous Republican administration is disgraced and the ideology of letting speculative markets rule is discredited by financial catastrophe. For the first time in four decades, a principled progressive enjoys an ideological tailwind.

An interesting straw in these shifting winds is a widely praised book by two young Republican strategists, Ross Douthat and Reihan Salam, titled *Grand New Party: How Republicans Can Win the Working Class and Save the American Dream*. Conservatives, these authors advise, need to stand for a socially conservative version of Roosevelt's New Deal. The conservative movement, they write:

> has missed opportunity after opportunity . . . by confusing being pro-market with being pro-business, by failing to distinguish between [government] spending that fosters dependency and spending that fosters independence and upward mobility . . . In the process, the Right has squandered the chance to forge a conservative class consciousness among working-class voters, a unity of political allegiance and socioeconomic identity that in its liberal form made the Roosevelt coalition so potent and enduring.

Alas, the social outlays actually proposed by Douthat and Salam—mostly tax credits—are at far too skimpy a scale to change the depressed economic horizons of working-class Americans. Republicans may embrace the rhetoric of Roosevelt when that seems convenient, but they never embrace the program. These authors' apt populist criticisms of big business simply would not fly with one major faction of the Republican Party, whose "conservative class consciousness" is primarily of the country-club class.

Yet the book was the object of a very favorable cover story in the flagship conservative magazine *The Weekly Standard*, and got laudatory blurbs from a galaxy of leading conservatives.

It is always the sign of the end of a political era when the formerly dominant party, in desperation, tries to copy the themes of the rising opposition party. And as feeble "New Democrats" found during the conservative epoch that stretched from Reagan to Bush II, the original is usually more persuasive than the imitation.

Transformation or Stagnation

The reader may still be wondering whether a program such as the one described in chapter 4 is either economically necessary or politically possible. A $600 billion net annual increase in federal spending? A crash program for energy self-sufficiency? Global regulation of finance? National health insurance? Would Obama really embrace any of this? Even if he did, he would face immense political obstacles. And surely there must be less utopian alternatives.

Roosevelt and LBJ both dreamed larger than the presumed political limits of their times. Mike Harrington, whose work inspired the Kennedy-Johnson War on Poverty, used to describe his reform program as the left wing of the possible. Measured against that standard, both the economic achievements of New Deal and the civil rights laws passed in the Johnson era were on the *far* left edge of the possible. Indeed, at the outset they were deemed beyond the realm of possibility entirely. The ideas discussed herein are rather less revolutionary than what either Roosevelt or Johnson accomplished—they just seem a little bit utopian because in our era expectations of government have been so diminished.

By now, I hope I have persuaded you that the economic conditions that Obama faces put him in an essentially similar historical situation, and that he has the capacity to transform the boundaries of what is conventionally thought politically achievable. But, yes, there are plenty of alternatives to the policies advanced in this book—just not very good ones. And the course of least resistance will be to pursue a more modest path.

Please recall that this book has distinguished between two kinds of challenges: emergency measures to brake a slide into depression; and treatment of more chronic conditions—a slow, relentless trajectory that has sundered the American middle class and menaced the planet. Both require ideological reversal, activist government, and uncommon leadership. But suppose Obama pursued a more cautious course.

On the recovery front, a failure to mount a program of large-scale public outlay would leave the economy in a self-deepening recession. And a program that continued the Bush administration's ad hoc bailouts of failing banks without radical regulatory reform would simply invite the next round of bubbles, crashes, and bailouts.

As financial conditions worsen and ordinary business profits dwindle, the economy goes into a classic, self-deepening downward spiral. This particular recession is more serious than most because it is compounded by three other convergent factors that undercut demand: the collapse of housing prices; increasing global inflation, which blunts the capacity of the Federal Reserve to use low interest rates to induce recovery; and the severe weakening of the financial sector. And this is on top of families and businesses that are already in debt to their limits.

The dynamics of "debt-deflation" are especially worrisome. In a classic paper published in 1933, the economist Irving Fisher described the difference between an ordinary business-cycle recession and a depression. A depression, Fisher explained, occurs when the value of assets falls below the value of debts against that asset. An example is a $300,000 house with a $400,000 mortgage.

In an era when worries have typically been more directed at inflation, it takes a little historic understanding to appreciate that deflation can also be a grave threat. When prices and wages fall, debts unfortunately remain constant—and consumers and businesses are overwhelmed by their debts. In the early and mid-1930s, the Roosevelt administration endeavored to brake falling prices, which were devastating farmers as well as ordinary businesses and homeowners. As prices fell, employers cut wages, depressing purchasing power and deepening the cycle.

Something similar occurred in Japan in the 1990s after a series of financial disasters not unlike the one we are now experiencing. Japan's central bank lowered the short-term interest rate all the way to zero in order to recapitalize banks and stimulate economic growth. But if businesses and homeowners expect falling prices, they won't borrow. In the 1930s, economists described the limitations of using interest-rate policy to cure deflation as "pushing on a string." Like so much else about the Great Depression, including the need for robust regulation of financial markets, deflation has been widely considered as a quaint bit of history not relevant for our own times.* But debt deflation, too, has returned.

In these circumstances, if Obama simply accepts conventional budgetary assumptions, he will not have adequate resources to counteract all the depressive tendencies assaulting the economy. The risk is that the recovery will remain weak, and we will be stuck at a plateau of high unemployment and falling real wages. As in the 1970s, it is entirely possible that sectoral inflation that has little to do with macroeconomic conditions will coexist with general deflation and recession.

People find themselves paying more for energy, food, and medical care, for reasons peculiar to those sectors and due to the weakness of the dollar, at the same time that general economic conditions are depressed. In these circumstances, the usual cure for inflation—slowing general economic growth or failing to stimulate it—would be entirely perverse. Instead, we need to

---

*One prescient exception was economist Paul Krugman's prophetic book on the risks of deflation, *The Return of Depression Economics*, published in 1999.

compensate for reduced private demand with increased public spending, while parallel initiatives reform health, energy, and food policy.

Besides a short-term recovery program based on public investment, this book has called for transformative structural reforms in labor-market and trade policy as well as health and energy. And here, too, there are more conventional alternatives—none of them very good. As we saw in chapter 3, if we continue the present system of fragmented and mostly private for-profit insurance, the result will be escalating medical inflation and increasing pressures to cap costs. This will end in a system in which only the affluent, who can pay the ever-higher out-of-pocket charges for treatments not covered by shrunken insurance, will get decent care.

The current energy path leads to ever-higher fuel prices and planetary calamity. Failure to radically change the current labor-market policies will lead to a continuation of widening job insecurity and income inequality. And tinkering with trade policy around the edges will lead to symbolic commitments on labor standards that do little to change the export of jobs, the widening trade imbalance, or the globalization of destabilizing financial speculation. That path, unfortunately, is the default path of a moderately liberal response. It just won't do the job.

Avoiding Legislative Impasse

Suppose Obama does embrace a transformative program. What are its political prospects? Here is where leadership makes all the difference.

Although it takes sixty votes in the Senate to break a filibuster, great presidents have demonstrated that a chief executive with a principled position, a compelling program, and a popular mandate can win over opposition votes. LBJ relied on moderate Republicans to enact civil rights laws over the objection of conservative Democrats, and then turned to racially conservative

Dixiecrats in his own party to pass Medicare over the protests of Republicans. Lincoln presided over a shifting coalition of Radical Republicans, more prudent Republicans, and moderate border-state and northern Democrats. One of the reasons he seemed to tack back and forth was precisely his need to hold that coalition together. But as he became a surer leader, he led and his "team of rivals" increasingly followed—as did the citizenry. George W. Bush achieved radical change with neither a popular mandate nor a realistic program, but on the basis of iron party discipline and the artifice of Karl Rove. His dwindling approval ratings demonstrate what happens when program, reality, and popular mandate diverge.

With close to sixty Democratic senators and an increased Democratic majority in the House, Obama will be able to win over Congress if he first wins over the country. That was the pattern with Franklin Roosevelt and Lyndon Johnson. It describes Lincoln and Theodore Roosevelt as well.

The numbers are also deceptive. Roosevelt, in his first term, when the famous First Hundred Days saw the most sweeping and breakneck enactment of legislation in American history, had just fifty-nine Democratic senators, only about the average of the past eight decades. Johnson had a bigger Senate Democratic majority of sixty-eight at its peak, though like Roosevelt, his nominal partisan majority included at least fifteen racially reactionary Dixiecrats who were a de facto third party inside the Democratic Party (many of whom also held key committee chairmanships).

By contrast, while today's congressional Democratic Party includes some economic centrists who are fiscally conservative and close to business lobbies, the most conservative Democratic senators—Mary Landrieu (Louisiana), Mark Pryor (Arkansas), Max Baucus (Minnesota), Ben Nelson (Nebraska), and Bill Nelson (Florida)—are somewhat to the left of the Dixiecrats that Roosevelt and Johnson had to reckon with. Even the fiscally conservative Blue Dogs are less anti-spending than anti-deficit. In a deep economic crisis, if most of the new spending is "paid for" by restoring taxes on the wealthy, at least some of the Blue Dogs could be won over.

Although the Bush-Rove-Norquist crowd did their best to drive progressive Republicans out of the GOP, there are still moderate Republicans eager to deliver something to their hard-pressed working- and middle-class constituents. In July 2008, when George W. Bush was equivocating on whether to veto the Frank-Dodd housing bill—a "big-government" measure (co-sponsored by Obama) needed to save hundreds of thousands of American homeowners from foreclosure—he was implored by several politically vulnerable Republican Senate and House incumbents to sign the bill. Ultimately, he relented, confronted by overwhelming bipartisan congressional unity. Likewise on the Democrats' 2008 bill to rein in privatization of Medicare, where Democrats called the Republicans' bluff and the bill passed by a veto-proof majority. The national agenda is looking more Democratic, both because the circumstances demand it and because Republican policies have so palpably failed.

As Obama has written,

> Not all Republican elected officials subscribe to the tenets of today's movement conservatives. In both the House and the Senate, and in state capitals across the country, there are those who cling to more traditional conservative values of temperance and restraint—men and women who recognize that piling up debt to finance tax cuts for the wealthy is irresponsible, that deficit-reduction can't take place on the backs of the poor, that separation of church and state protects church as well as state, that conservation and conservatism don't have to conflict, and that foreign policy should be based on facts and not on wishful thinking.

Bringing Republicans into a progressive policy consensus that Obama leads has been has been an Obama trademark ever since he went to Springfield, Illinois, as a young state senator in 1997. This is what he accomplished as a lead sponsor of landmark legislation to reform the Illinois criminal justice system, including several initially controversial measures such as mandatory videotaping of confessions. Obama just kept working until he had built a consensus, and he did this during a period when the Democrats were the minority party in the state senate. This mode of leadership is what LBJ achieved and what George W. Bush promised as a candidate ("a uniter, not a divider") but quickly abandoned in office.

The hunger for a president who heals divisions and solves national problems is palpable both in the electorate and in the commentariat. There is no doubt that Obama will seek to build the national unity that Bush falsely pledged, but from the reverse side of the spectrum. The intriguing question is whether he will attempt it as an LBJ-style economic progressive, or as a Bill Clinton–style centrist. Reading Obama's own speeches and writings, one can find tantalizing evidence of both impulses. But it is far more likely that he will govern as a progressive, both because of his own convictions and the demands of the times.

Coming to the Aid of the Party

As James MacGregor Burns has observed, the great presidents were also great party builders. In our constitutional system, with its structural bias against activist government, Burns notes that it takes strong parties to bridge over "the fragmentation inherent in checks and balances and in federalism," to allow administrations to enact their programs.

What is a political party, anyway? Another eminent political scientist, V. O. Key Jr., distinguished between the institutional party, the party-in-government, and the party in the electorate. Shrewd presidents have built all three. The institutional party is the machinery that rings doorbells, recruits and trains candidates, registers voters, and gets out the vote. Ideally, it is active both during and between campaigns. The party-in-government is the alliance, weak or strong, between the chief executive and his floor leaders and back-benchers in Congress who either support or frustrate his program. And the party in the electorate is the partisan self-identification of voters.

The conventional view in recent years has been that partisanship is evaporating, but the reality is more complex and instructive. It's true that more voters list themselves as independents. But all three forms of party have been disproportionately weakened *on the Democratic side*. Reagan and Bush II, with the aid of operatives like Lee Atwater and Karl Rove, strengthened both the institutional Republican Party and the Republican party-in-government (which, for Bush's first seven years, was slavishly loyal to the White House). The last two Democratic presidents, by contrast, often seemed to be running against their party. Their political organizations were more personalist than party-based. Lists of voters and donors were treated as proprietary, and had to be rebuilt from scratch by succeeding candidates.

A new wrinkle that intensified this problem was the proliferation of so-called Section 527 organizations, which were created to take advantage of a loophole in the campaign finance laws. While federal law limits the amount of money that a campaign can collect from an individual, the Supreme Court has held that political donations are tantamount to free speech and there is no limit to the amount a person may spend to express an idea. So if a person wants to contribute unlimited sums to nominally independent organizations to spread the word that McCain is a patriot and Obama is a terrorist, there is no legal obstacle so long as there is no institutional connection to an electoral campaign. In recent years, the nastiest negative campaigning, such as the "Swift Boat" slanders of John Kerry, has been done under the auspices of independent Section 527 committees so that the candidate could claim plausible deniability. (*Section 527* refers to the provision of the IRS Code that governs such outlays.)

On the Democratic side, very wealthy donors have heavily used

527s to raise and spend money to register voters, build sophisticated voter analysis and targeting software, and get out the vote. The largest of the Section 527 groups on the Democratic side, America Coming Together (ACT) and its sister organization, the Media Fund, together raised $196.4 million for voter drives and an ad blitz. Thanks to these donations, John Kerry's hapless 2004 campaign was at least financially and technologically competitive (the problem was not money; it was the candidate and his handlers).

The original idea was that these groups would be part of the permanent liberal infrastructure. But after Kerry's demoralizing defeat, the wealthy liberals who put up much of the money for the Democratic 527s abruptly closed up shop in July 2005. As entrepreneurs, they just bailed out of a losing bet. This is the hazard of building up political structures parallel to the institutional party—and of relying on the caprices of a few wealthy liberals. As a consequence, the Democratic Party did not inherit all the valuable campaign assets of all this costly campaign technology electioneering.

Incredibly, the single most valuable asset of the Democratic 527s, the carefully coded master donor lists, had to be sold to a private businessman. He turned out to be a longtime political operative-cum-entrepreneur named Harold Ickes, the son of FDR's secretary of the interior. Ickes bought the lists, promising to maintain them, enhance them, and rent them on an arm's-length basis to any willing Democrat. It made some Democrats more than a little nervous that Ickes was also a senior strategist to Hillary Clinton.

Nothing like this happened on the Republican side, where the institutional party is the custodian of lists and targeting technology. Unlike among the Democrats, where the entire machinery needs to be reinvented almost from scratch for every presidential campaign, Republicans enjoy a much stronger institutional party, nationally and at the state and local levels. Operatives like Karl Rove have great ideological respect for private entrepreneurs—but know that party politics is too important to leave to businessmen.

As basically anti-party men, presidents such as Clinton and Carter weakened their own capacity to deliver—and strengthened the opposition party by becoming reliant on its votes, its ideology, or both. Triangulation may have helped Clinton personally, but by disparaging his own party and its core worldview, Clinton's strategy helped set up the Democrats for a defeat in 2000, a year of peace and prosperity that should have produced a strong Democratic win. Like Typhoid Mary, Clinton survived while infecting his community.

Against this depressing background, Barack Obama is a welcome reversion—a party builder. Like the current national Democratic Party chairman, Howard Dean, Obama committed himself to a fifty-state strategy, rather than writing off states that were heavily Republican. This commitment both reflects Obama's own core beliefs as one who looks beyond the artificial construct of Red States and Blue ones—and also turns out to be smart tactics. His unorthodox strategy made all the difference in allowing Obama to win the Democratic nomination. He built his margins in primaries and caucuses in majority-Republican states, places that Hillary Clinton's campaign was more likely to write off.

Obama has built on Dean's strategy of investing in party infrastructure and candidates rarely paid attention by the national party—candidates for "down-ticket" offices such as state rep and county commissioner. The Democrats' pickup of thirty-one House seats in 2006, many of them in "Red" states, reflected not just a popular repudiation of Bush but also the Democrats' investment in states where their candidates seldom win. This accelerated in 2008, with Obama's strong support.

As Dana Goldstein and Ezra Klein have observed, Obama is in some ways the accidental beneficiary of Dean's party building, but he and his team "understand the moment's promise and chose a strategy capable of fulfilling it." Obama also has a shrewd grasp of the twenty-first-century form of grassroots activism—the Internet.

The other factor that made the difference in Obama's nomination victory was his astonishing success in motivating voters and raising small sums of money from a huge number of new donors, using networking techniques pioneered by organizations such as MoveOn.org. Hillary Clinton's strategy for locking up the nomination early was to assemble an overwhelming lead in money and in endorsements. It turned out to be hopelessly last-century. Coming out of nowhere, Obama quickly matched and then surpassed her money advantage. He did this partly because he inspired a huge grassroots network of people both to embrace his candidacy and to contribute small sums, and partly because his more professional fund-raisers were far more Internet-savvy than Clinton's.

My former *American Prospect* colleague, Josh Green, writing in the *Atlantic Monthly* ("The Amazing Money Machine," June 2008), tells the fascinating story of how several of Obama's early group of large donors and fund-raisers were politically liberal Silicon Valley entrepreneurs—people with great facility for the technology, subculture, and business strategy of "viral" networking. Like the legions of younger Obama kids, these professionals understood the world of MySpace and Facebook. As entrepreneurs, they had developed successful business models for software, based on Internet marketing. So they were perfectly positioned to consummate a rendezvous with Obama's inspired amateurs—the millions of ordinary citizens and bloggers who had grown up as users of the Internet. Obama, a onetime community organizer, far surpassed Hillary Clinton's in grasping the potential of the 'Net-roots as a twenty-first-century medium of politics and engaged citizenship.

At the same time, Obama has not fled from the traditional party machinery. Unlike Clinton and Carter, who were far more personalist, Obama turned to competent party people in building his own staff. He is extremely close to former Senate majority leader Tom Daschle, and hired Daschle's most effective aide, Pete Rouse, to be his own chief of staff. Rouse, in turn, brought in other veterans. Carter and Clinton, by contrast, relied on outsiders even after winning the White House. Neither was well loved by Democrats in Congress, and their legislative programs suffered. Obama is turning out to be that rarest of Democratic presidential candidates, a charismatic innovator who is also a party man.

The Audacity of Democratic Citizenship

This successful campaign strategy is very likely to carry over into an era of both party building and the use of presidential leadership and affirmative government to revive affirmative citizenship. I mentioned the pervasive myth that individual initiative and government help are somehow at odds. A related myth is that effective government stifles effective citizenship. Liberal Democrats, according to conservative authors Douthat and Salam, want to "emphasize dependence over self-sufficiency and bureaucratic condescension over self-help." Their tools, supposedly, are "ever-larger bureaucracy and ever-greater federal power." Other conservative writers have associated localism and libertarianism with a revival of small-d democracy.

But if you consult the historical experience, expansion of democracy and effectiveness of government have gone hand in hand. The periods of activist government were precisely those of enhanced citizenship. Roosevelt did not just deliver assistance. He asked for the people's help and devised ways of engaging people. The WPA and so many other innovations of the Roosevelt era were mechanisms for connecting people with their government. Lyndon Johnson acquired his empathy for the struggles of destitute Mexican Americans as the Texas director of FDR's National Youth Administration, which gave young people jobs. During World War II, ordinary people contributed to the war effort in countless ways. While my father was landing in Normandy, my mother volunteered as a rooftop civil defense spotter on the lookout for German bombers—which never came, but we didn't know that at the time. And this spirit was not just wartime solidarity. It began with Roosevelt's first Fireside Chat.

Geoffrey Nunberg quotes an emblematic passage from the 1940 movie version of John Steinbeck's *Grapes of Wrath*, in which Tom Joad and his family, having finally made it to California in their jalopy, come upon a relief camp and are astonished as the caretaker describes what is on offer:

> Tom: You got dances, too?
> Caretaker: We got the best dances in the county every Saturday night.
> Tom: Say, who runs this place?
> Caretaker: The government.

In the Roosevelt era, government actually delivered and the people reciprocated. The iconic series of four Norman Rockwell posters illustrating Roosevelt's Four Freedoms shows people freed from want, sitting around a Thanksgiving turkey dinner, but also an ordinary citizen at a town meeting—not just expressing freedom of speech to say his piece, but encouraged to believe that his speaking can make a difference. Effective government and engaged citizens enhance each other.

In a period like our own, where elections can be stolen and government fails to deliver help even in the face of a catastrophe like Hurricane Katrina, anger and frustration quickly give way to resignation and cynical passivity. Of course politicians are crooks; of course the government never showed up to help—what did you expect? In the New Orleans tragedy, ordinary citizens heroically did their part. The Bush administration just failed to reciprocate.

A caring and competent government could have rallied far more local energy. Americans are great community-builders, and most cynics are frustrated idealists. Give us a leader who revives American traditions at more than the level of slogan, rekindles our higher aspirations, and delivers practical help—and the civic impulse revives. Right after 9/11, many commentators predicted a new era of solidarity and shared sacrifice for the common good. It never happened, because Bush never called on the people.

Not surprisingly, eras of effective government are also times of rising voter participation. The increase in voter turnout in 1936 over 1932 broke all previous records. After Lyndon Johnson began delivering on the deferred New Deal agenda in 1964, turnout sharply increased in the election that November, and not just among blacks (most of whom still could not vote in the Deep South). Conversely, the disastrous policy choices of Johnson's war, Nixon's corruption, and Carter's fecklessness depressed both expectations and participation. The dramatically increased political engagement in the 2008 campaign, especially among energized young voters who have never before seen this kind of practical idealism close up, will continue into the Obama presidency. If Obama doesn't let them down, they will become an engaged political generation of the sort that we haven't seen in many decades.

In addition to enhancing civic participation via both inspirational leadership and practical help, there is a long-deferred list of necessary measures to remove obstacles to participation and welcome people into the voting both. Our election administration is an embarrassing crazy quilt of underfunded state and local jurisdictions. No wonder the private election-machine industry ran roughshod with unreliable products after the 2000 debacle. We need a real federal agency, with the authority to set high and uniform national standards, the technological competence to assure reliable voting systems, and the funding needed to assist states in the changes they will need to make.

These reforms could include eliminating arbitrary deadlines and allowing Election Day registration; allowing pre-registration of all high school students; reforming laws that make permanent nonvoting outcasts of people coming out of prison; ensuring accurate lists without onerous ID requirements; and allowing voters maximum opportunities to vote through early voting and more use of vote-by-mail. All would help bring people into the process. Electoral reform has been blocked in Congress, but a president who believed in expanding and deepening our democracy could preside over an era of democratic renewal. The entire psychology is circular. Competent government and engagement of the people restores faith in the enterprise of government, and in turn restores the civic impulse.

There are two complementary strategies for enhancing citizenship. One is reducing barriers and welcoming people into the process of participation; the other is giving them a reason to participate. More than a decade ago, there was great enthusiasm for the new invention of the "Motor Voter" law signed by President Clinton in 1993. This law promotes voter registration at motor vehicle bureaus, welfare offices, and other retail government agencies. My friend Marshall Ganz, former director of organizing for the national farmworkers union, wrote an article for *The American Prospect* whose title says it all: "Motor Voter or Motivated Voter?" Easing the process of registration is enhanced when people feel they have a reason to vote. At this writing, Marshall Ganz is director of organizer training for Barack Obama.

One other conservative slander is the right-wing claim that liberal, bureaucratic "big government" crowds out forms of government that are closer to the people. The fact is that a great deal of federal aid necessarily is channeled through state and local governments—which have been starved during the past three decades by Republican taxing and spending priorities. Conversely, with Republicans controlling Washington, some of the most effective progressive initiatives have been launched at the state and local level—everything from living-wage laws to strategies for environmentally friendly "smart growth." As Washington has become an all-purpose commercial against government, there has been an offsetting profusion of inventiveness at the local level. The environmental movement is the quintessential example of bottom-up activism.

Meanwhile, in one of the riper forms of hypocrisy, the right wing has abandoned its principled support for states' rights in favor of a doctrine of opportunistic federal preemption. In a vacuum of federal stewardship, as states and localities have become leaders in consumer protection as well as financial and environmental standards, the Bush administration used its congressional majority and its lock on the courts to preempt one area of regulatory policy after another.

An administration that respects the possibilities of government can get this balance between federal and local government right. The federal government can provide adequate resources while energizing levels of government closest to the people, and allowing state or local governments to provide protections beyond federal minimums if they so choose.

Imagine what we as a nation of citizens might do if the federal government were ally rather than roadblock. The people are ready to support an activist president if he asks something of them, as Lincoln, Roosevelt, and Johnson did. And just as our next president needs to ask more of us, we need to ask more of ourselves as citizens—and of him. Revival of civic life can be a virtuous circle.

As Lincoln and Roosevelt taught us, leadership is not a one-way street. An activated citizenry is not just a passive army of political supporters who will cheer and vote on cue. That describes the role of the people under fascism or communism—armies of human props. We got a whiff of that kind of stagecraft when President Bush gave his famous and premature Mission Accomplished speech of May 1, 2003, using the crew of the USS *Abraham Lincoln* for their production values.

But in a vibrant democracy, the people keep their leaders honest. That is the whole point. The 8,000 daily letters Roosevelt began receiving from his first day in office were not just thank-you notes. The people had ideas, and complaints, and yearnings. Leadership can signal that it is listening—or just manipulating. Bush followed by Obama could be one of the greatest contrasts in presidential leadership of all time.

When Obama went through his three weeks of midsummer straying to the political center-right, he heard from his supporters, big-time. Effective governance invites feedback from the people. Obama, let's recall, got his start in politics as a community organizer. His assignment was to conduct twenty to thirty interviews a day, to find out what was on people's minds. The first (and second, and third) qualification for an effective community organizer is a gift for active listening. Obama honed this natural talent around the kitchen tables of Chicago's South Side. It's a basic qualification for a transformative president as well.

And so America waits. What will become of our economy, our society, our nation, and our children? What sort of a leader will our next president be, at this perilous and promising moment? Never in my political lifetime has more apprehension come bundled with more hope. I leave the last words to Barack Obama. "The true test of the American ideal is whether we're able to recognize our failings and then rise together to meet the challenges of our time. Whether we allow ourselves to be shaped by events and history, or whether we act to shape them."

Afterword and Acknowledgments

This book began with the germ of an idea for a magazine article. In the fall of 2007, I had just published a book warning of impending financial collapse (and none too soon) called *The Squandering of America*. Barack Obama was starting to look like he could be more than just a fresh face.

I realized that by January 2009 there could be a rendezvous of a perilous economic moment with a new leader and an ideological reversal. I began reading more about great American presidents—leaders whom I thought of as transformational. I saw evidence that Obama might have the makings of such a leader. And I sought to enlist the presidential historian whom I most admired, Doris Kearns Goodwin, to write a feature article on this theme for the magazine that I co-edit, *The American Prospect*.

Doris, as it turned out, was busy researching her latest book, on Theodore Roosevelt. But she agreed to take time for an interview. She is the rare interviewee who speaks something close to finished prose. We spoke for three hours, and ended up publishing an edited transcript of the conversation in the January 2008 issue of *The American Prospect* (see www.prospect.org/cs/articles?article=a_conversation_with_doris_kearns_goodwin_).

The more I thought about the subject, and about the transformational potential of Barack Obama in a deepening economic crisis, the more I felt that the subject was worth a book. I suggested to Doris that perhaps she might write it, but she tossed the idea back to me and generously offered to suggest sources and read chapters.

I owe a huge debt to Doris, and to other great historians whom I read or reread, especially James MacGregor Burns, William Leuchtenburg, Arthur Schlesinger Jr., Taylor Branch, and Nick Kotz; to the political scientist Rick Valelly; and to two other scholars of the New Deal, journalist Jonathan Alter and legal historian Joel Seligman.

It turned out that Professor Burns was writing about "transforming" presidential leadership long before I addressed the subject. Many of his concepts and insights enrich this book. On the eve of his ninetieth birthday, he generously agreed to read my chapters.

Others who helped inspire and inform this work, or who read draft chapters, include Miles Rapoport, Michael Lipsky, Mark Schmitt, David Smith, Patrick Bresette, and my wife, Joan Fitzgerald, who read every word of multiple drafts, taking time away from her own writing and her garden, and from what was originally planned as a working vacation.

I am grateful to all of my colleagues at *The American Prospect*, where many of my writings have appeared. Since Paul Starr, Bob Reich, and I founded the *Prospect* in 1989, our purpose has been to reclaim and redeem the liberal project. Thanks to colleagues Harold Meyerson, Ezra Klein, Ann Friedman, Dorian Friedman, Joby Gelbspan, Emily Parsons, Diane Straus Tucker, and Ben Taylor. Short portions of this book appeared in different form in two *Prospect* articles. I have also adapted portions of two other pieces that appeared in *Foreign Affairs* and in *The New England Journal of Medicine*.

I also want to acknowledge my many other colleagues at Demos beyond those named here. Demos is a uniquely valuable think tank, whose whole reason for being is to connect the dots that link a strong democracy, an effective government, and a just society. That is precisely what our next president needs to do.

Special thanks also to Bernard Rapoport for his support for this and others of my books, and to Bill Moyers.

This has also been a remarkable publishing experience, thanks to the innovators at Chelsea Green and to Hendrik Hertzberg, Richard Parker, and Peter Dreier. When I began the book, I had tentatively decided to take a big risk and write most of it before we knew who had won the election. The idea was that we would then roll the presses right after Election Day, and get it into print around January assuming that Obama won—otherwise, have a manuscript bonfire.

Then Margo Baldwin, the president of Chelsea Green, and I had the same idea almost simultaneously. Why not take an even bigger risk and publish by Labor Day in time for the fall campaign, on the premise that Obama would win? Talk about the audacity of hope!

Along the way, Margo and her team invented new strategies of publishing, working with Amazon and other business partners, which allowed us to deliver finished books from copy editor to reader in just three weeks. I suspect that traditional publishers, whose nine-month production schedules are more in the nineteenth century than the twenty-first, will eventually follow suit, or lose authors to innovators.

So this book has been transformative in this unanticipated respect as well. Heartfelt thanks to Margo, to my superb editor Joni Praded, astute copyeditor Laura Jorstad, and to publicist Katharine Walton, project manager Emily Foote, and proofreader Bill Bokermann; to my agent John Brockman who introduced me to Chelsea Green; to our publicists at Demos, Tim Rusch and Gennady Kolker; and to the entire Chelsea Green team.

I only hope that my experience with our next president will be as good as my experience with Chelsea Green. And I hope, immodestly, that this book will also make a difference in how we think about the presidency and the moment.

Endnotes

v **"That people can be lifted"** James MacGregor Burns, *Leadership* (New York: Harper and Row, 1978), 462.

1. A Great President or a Failed One

3 **"History suggests that unless"** "A Conversation with Doris Kearns Goodwin," *American Prospect*, January–February 2008.

7 **"At the highest stage"** Burns, *Leadership*, 24.

7 **"I saw John Kennedy"** David Mandell, *Obama: From Promise to Power* (New York: Amistad/HarperCollins, 2007), 377.

8 **"I imagine the white southerner"** Barack Obama, *The Audacity of Hope* (New York: Crown Publishers, 2006), 42.

10 **"We're beginning to understand"** *The Wall Street Journal*, July 2, 2008, A12.

11 **"Senator Obama is not just tacking"** *The New York Times*, July 8, 2008, 17.

11 **Hendrik Hertzberg, in a close analysis** Hendrik Hertzberg, "Flip-Flop Flap," *The New Yorker*, July 21, 2008, www.newyorker.com/talk/comment/2008/07/21/080721taco_talk_hertzberg.

11 **"I am a Democrat"** Obama, *Audacity of Hope*, 10.

12 **"Depending on your tastes"** *Ibid.*, 24.

13 **"We know that our health-care system"** *Ibid.*, 23.

14 **"Imagine, for a moment"** Obama foreign policy speech, July 15, 2008. See www.nytimes.com/2008/07/15/us/politics/15text-obama.html.

15 **"Obama's rise has often appeared"** www.newyorker.com/reporting/2008/07/21/080721fa_fact_lizza.

15 **"Chance, positioning, and managerial strategy"** Doris Kearns Goodwin, *Team of Rivals* (New York: Simon & Schuster, 2005), 250.

17 **columnist Frank Rich wondered** www.nytimes.com/2008/07/27/opinion/27rich.html.

23 **These "wealth effects"** Dean M. Maki and Michael G. Palumbo, "Disentangling the Wealth Effect: A Cohort Analysis of Household Saving in the 1990s," www.federalreserve.gov/pubs/feds/2001/200121/200121abs.html.

23 **According to a technical study** Alan Greenspan and James Kennedy, "Sources and Uses of Equity Extracted from Homes," www.federalreserve.gov/pubs/feds/2007/200720/200720pap.pdf.

25 **"An Agenda for Middle Class Success"** www.obamamagazine.com/obama-issues/an-agenda-for-middle-class-success-barack-obama-in-st-louis-missouri.

26 **Obama proposed a much bolder $50 billion** www.scribd.com/doc/4385783/Barack-Obamas-Emergency-Economic-Plan

29 **at least $300 billion of taxes** See Max Sawicki, ed., *Bridging the Tax Gap* (Washington, D.C.: Economic Policy Institute, 2006).

30 **three articles from the front page** *The New York Times*, July 2, 2008.

31 **"Our history should give us confidence"** http://en.wikisource.org/wiki/U.S._Economy_Speech.

34 **"With public sentiment, nothing can fail"** Goodwin, *Team of Rivals*, 206.

2. How Transformative Presidents Lead

35 **"I mean by leadership"** James MacGregor Burns, *The Power to Lead* (New York: Simon & Schuster, 1984), 16.

35 **"Our critical situation is chiefly due"** Demosthesnes, quoted in Arthur Schlesinger Jr., *Kennedy or Nixon: Does it Make a Difference?* (New York: Macmillan, 1960), i.

36 **in 1860 Lincoln was not yet** "A Conversation with Doris Kearns Goodwin."

36 **the 4-P's Candidate** James MacGregor Burns, *Roosevelt: The Lion and the Fox* (New York: Harvest, Harcourt, Brace and World, 1956), 133.

36 **"a chameleon on Scotch plaid"** Kenneth S. Davis, *FDR: The New York Years* (New York: Random House 1965), 362.

37 **"Governments can err"** Franklin Delano Roosevelt, speech to the Democratic National Convention, Philadelphia, June 27, 1936.

37 **"I accuse the present"** William Leuchtenburg, *Franklin Roosevelt and the New Deal, 1932–1940* (New York: Harper and Row/Harper Torchbooks, 1963), 11.

38 **"Given later developments"** Marriner Eccles, *Beckoning Frontiers*, p. 95, quoted in Leuchtenburg, *Franklin Roosevelt and the New Deal.*

38 **"Under the leadership of Franklin Roosevelt"** Leuchtenberg, *Franklin Roosevelt and the New Deal*, 45.

38 **3 billion trees** Jonathan Alter, *The Defining Moment* (New York: Simon & Schuster Paperbacks, 2006), 299.

39 **"Just deny you were ever"** *Ibid.*, 276.

40 **fewer banks failed during the entire** *Ibid.*, 60.

40 **In his first radio address** www.fdrlibrary.marist.edu/031233.html.

43 **"President Roosevelt has done his part"** Leuchtenburg, *Franklin Roosevelt and the New Deal*, 47.

45 **"Hell, what's the presidency for?"** Merle Miller, *Lyndon: An Oral Biography* (New York: G. P. Putnam's Sons, 1980), 337, cited in Nick Kotz, *Judgment Days* (Boston: Houghton Mifflin, 2005), 22.

46 **"The whites think we're just"** Taylor Branch, *Pillar of Fire* (New York: Simon & Schuster, 1998), 94

46 **civil rights bill was widely considered** Kotz, *Judgment Days*, 8, 14.

47 **"No memorial oration or eulogy"** Lyndon Johnson, Address to Joint Session of Congress, November 27, 1963, www.lbjlib.utexas.edu/Johnson/archives.hom/speeches.hom/631127.asp.

48 **"I'm not going to cavil"** Branch, *Pillar of Fire*, 187.

50 **"At times, history . . . we shall overcome"** www.lbjlib.utexas.edu/johnson/archives.hom/speeches.hom/650315.asp.

54 **"We had to struggle with"** www.fdrlibrary.marist.edu/od2ndst.html.

56 **"I want to speak to you"** http://millercenter.org/scripps/archive/speeches/detail/3402.

57 **"His Administration attested not so much"** Burns, *Power to Lead*, 32.

60 **"Leaders, whatever their professions"** *Ibid.*, 39.

61 **"It is my conviction that"** Goodwin, *Team of Rivals*, 502–503.

62 **"As a politician, he had an intuitive"** *Ibid.*, 501.

63 **The political scientist Richard Valelly** Richard M. Valelly, *The Two Reconstructions* (Chicago: University of Chicago Press, 2004).

65 **"Roosevelt's success in mobilizing the nation"** Doris Kearns Goodwin, *No Ordinary Time* (New York: Simon & Schuster, 1994), 608.

65 "The peace-loving nations . . . joins in a quarantine" www.vlib.us/amdocs/ texts/fdrquarn.html.

66 "It is a terrible thing" Cited in Burns, *Roosevelt: The Lion and the Fox*, 319.

66 A Gallup poll showed Leuchtenburg, *Franklin Roosevelt and the New Deal*, 293.

67 "the most dictatorial and arbitrary" Cited in *National War Powers Commission Report* (Charlottesville: University of Virginia, Miller Center, 2008), 29. See http://millercenter.org/dev/ci/system/application/views/_newwebsite/ policy/commissions/warpowers/report.pdf.

67 "For Roosevelt, the destroyer deal" Burns, *Roosevelt: The Lion and the Fox*, 441.

68 "The Nazi masters of Germany" www.fdrlibrary.marist.edu/122940.html.

69 "We have just now engaged" www.mtholyoke.edu/acad/intrel/WorldWar2/ fdr24.htm.

70 According to Robert Schlesinger's recent book Robert Schlesinger, *White House Ghosts* (New York: Simon & Schuster, 2008), 275.

71 publish a front-page story *The New York Times*, July 10, 1968.

71 "I don't oppose all wars" http://en.wikisource.org/wiki/ Barack_Obama%27s_Iraq_Speech.

72 since James MacGregor Burns described Congress's James MacGregor Burns, *Deadlock of Democracy* (New York: Prentice Hall, 1963).

73 "In the hands of a truly" Goodwin, *Team of Rivals*, xvii.

3. Audacity Versus Undertow

74 "There go my people" See www.britannica.com/EBchecked/topic/334511/ Alexandre-Auguste-Ledru-Rollin.

74 "Worldly wisdom teaches us" John Maynard Keynes, *The General Theory of Employment, Interest and Money* (New York: Harcourt, Brace and Jovanovich, 1936, 1964), 158.

74 "My hope is that people" *The New York Times*, July 16, 2008, 1.

79 "In January, I met with" See www.macfound.org/site/apps/nlnet/content3.as px?c=lkLXJ8MQKrH&b=2578111&content_id=%.

80 "I would ask that if you" See www.pgpf.org/newsroom/oped/pgphouse.

80 Peterson himself put the unfunded liability Peter G. Peterson, *Facing Up* (New York: Simon & Schuster, 1993).

82 The ensuing alarmist joint statement See www.brookings.edu/~/media/Files/ rc/papers/2008/04_fiscal_future/04_fiscal_future.pdf.

83 "The authors agree that certain myths" Some of this language has since been removed from the Heritage Web site. The sanitized version can be found at www.heritage.org/Research/Budget/wp0408.cfm.

84 "jeopardize the health and economic security" See www.brookings.edu/ papers/2008/07_fiscal_responsibility_aaron.aspx.

85 "Right now, thanks to the current" See www.brookings.edu/articles/2008/ summer_social-investments_sawhill.aspx.

85 "about at their postwar average" See www.urban.org/UploadedPDF/901038_ Reischauer_FiscalChallenges.pdf.

87 "Government cannot solve our problems" www.jimmycarterlibrary.org/docu- ments/speeches/su78jec.phtml.

88 "We know big government does not" www.cnn.com/US/9601/budget/01-27/ clinton_radio.

88 "In this present crisis" www.reaganlibrary.com/reagan/speeches/first.asp.

89 **"The Democrats' big mistake"**   Geoffrey Nunberg, "Thinking About the Government," *American Prospect*, May 2005. See www.prospect.org/cs/articles?article=thinking_about_the_government_041905.

90 **"Alongside our famous individualism"**   http://en.wikisource.org/wiki/2004_Democratic_National_Convention_keynote_address.

91 **"For a very long time now"**   See www.boston.com/news/local/massachusetts/articles/2007/01/04/text_of_governor_deval_l_patricks_inaugural_address.

91 **"Let's fulfill the Colorado Promise"**   See www.thecherrycreeknews.com/content/view/947/2.

92 **"Throughout American history"**   http://democraticgovernors.org/content/523/pennsylvania-gov-ed-rendells-speech-dec-1-2005.

93 **A fine example is political scientist**   Paul C. Light, *Government's Greatest Achievements* (Washington, D.C.: Brookings Institution Press, 2002).

97 **Consider, for example, an extensive**   www.thirdway.org/data/product/file/128/Third_Way_-_Playing_Offense_on_Taxes.pdf.

97 **Blueprint for Change, the campaign's basic**   www.barackobama.com/pdf/ObamaBlueprintForChange.pdf.

100 **"How selfish soever man may be"**   Adam Smith, *The Theory of Moral Sentiments* (Amherst, N.Y.: Prometheus Books, 1759, 2000), 3.

101 **I accepted an invitation to testify**   www.house.gov/apps/list/hearing/financial-svcs_dem/testimony_-_kuttner.pdf.

102 **"We are in a worldwide crisis"**   www.washingtonpost.com/wp-dyn/content/article/2008/07/10/AR2008071002264.html.

107 **His name was Drew Westen**   Drew Westen, *The Political Brain* (New York: Public Affairs, 2007).

108 **Amy Sullivan published one**   www.washingtonmonthly.com/features/2005/0501.sullivan.html.

110 **"The first . . . takes a positive approach"**   www.democracycorps.com/focus/2007/07/frustration-demand-for-change-continue-to-grow-2/?section=Analysis - 27k.

113 **economist Stephen Rose contended**   Stephen Rose, "The Trouble with Class-Interest Populism," www.ppionline.org/documents/Class-Interest_Populism_042606.pdf.

113 **Mark Penn repeatedly counseled**   Mark Penn, "But Only with the Right Agenda," *Blueprint Magazine*, September 26, 2002.

115 **"My friends, as our nation"**   This medley is drawn mainly from Obama's Knox College commencement address of June 4, 2005, and his Cooper Union address of March 27, 2008. Knox College: en.wikisource.org/wiki/Comfmencement_Address%2C_Knox_College_2005. Cooper Union speech: http://en.wikisource.org/wiki/U.S._Economy_Speech.

4. Repairing a Damaged Economy

121 **"Make no small plans"**   http://en.wikipedia.org/wiki/Daniel_Burnham.

123 **"A National Infrastructure Reinvestment Bank"**   www.cfr.org/publication/16018/obamas_speech_on_manufacturing_and_trade.html.

124 **"State Growth Fund to prevent"**   www.scribd.com/doc/4385783/Barack-Obamas-Emergency-Economic-Plan

126 **"This morning you announced a new"**   http://m.npr.org/news.jsp?key=412852&rc=po&p=0.

128 **The Congressional Budget Office estimates that** www.cbo.gov/ftpdocs/93xx/ doc9366/Senate_Housing.pdf.

132 **"We have moved from a"** http://econclubny.org/files/Transcript_Volcker_ April_2008.pdf.

137 **"There have long been clear rules"** *The New York Times*, July 16, 2008.

141 **"The banks are too big"** *The New York Times*, July 20, 2008.

154 **I published my findings in the** Robert Kuttner, "The Copenhagen Consensus," *Foreign Affairs*, March–April 2008.

159 **And as economist Alan Blinder** Alan S. Blinder, "Outsourcing: Bigger than You Thought," *American Prospect*, November 2006. See www.prospect.org/cs/ articles?article=outsourcing_bigger_than_you_thought.

159 **"We're borrowing money from China"** www.npr.org/templates/story/story. php?storyId=92635699#92638501.

164 **The Apollo Alliance for Renewable Energy** www.apolloalliance.org/ resources_tenpointplan.php.

164 **According to testimony by Daniel Kammen** http://epw.senate.gov/public/ index.cfm?FuseAction=Hearings.Testimony&Hearing_ID=1b098dbe-802a-23 ad-4c56-7889bcbf2eb8&Witness_ID=6b35c1de-a5c7-4cc7-b93d-02731b8cf095.

166 **His energy proposals, released August 4** www.barackobama.com/issues/energy.

169 **Reputable researchers calculate** See Sharon Brownlee, *Overtreated: How Too Much Medicine Is Making Us Sicker and Poorer* (New York: Bloomsbury Group, 2007).

170 **the gap between generalist and specialist** American Medical Group Association, "2007 Medical Group Compensation and Financial Survey."

173 **"The truth is, trade is here"** www.barackobama.com/2008/04/14/remarks_ for_senator_barack_oba_5.php.

176 **James Gustave Speth, one of the** James Gustave Speth, *The Bridge at the End of the World* (New Haven, Conn.: Yale University Press, 2008).

5. A Work in Progress

180 **The sociologist and commentator Amitai Etzioni** www.huffingtonpost.com/ authorarchive/?amitai-etzioni/2008/07.

181 **Bartlett quotes Christine Allison** www.tnr.com/story_print. html?id=46a816dc-f843-41ec-9fe4-fbeac17bcfca.

181 **When he joined a weekly poker game** Mandell, *From Promise to Power*, 123.

181 **the wide availability of prostitutes** *Ibid.*, 160.

183 **"has missed opportunity after opportunity"** Ross Douthat and Reihan Salam, *Grand New Party: How Republicans Can Win the Working Class and Save the American Dream* (New York: Doubleday, 2008), 11.

185 **A depression, Fisher explained** Irving Fisher, "The Debt Deflation Theory of Great Depressions," *Econometrica* 1 (1933).

189 **"Not all Republican elected officials"** Obama, *Audacity of Hope*, 37.

190 **"the fragmentation inherent"** Burns, *The Power to Lead*, 135.

193 **As Dana Goldstein and Ezra Klein have observed** Dana Goldstein and Ezra Klein, "It's His Party," *The American Prospect*, September 2008, 17

194 **several of Obama's early group** Josh Green, "The Amazing Money Machine," *Atlantic*, June 2008.

195 **"emphasize dependence over self-sufficiency"** Douthat and Salam, *Grand New Party*, 10.

195 **Geoffrey Nunberg quotes an emblematic passage** Nunberg, "Thinking About the Government."

198 **invention of the "Motor Voter" law** Marshall Ganz, "Motor Voter or Motivated Voter?" *American Prospect*, November 30, 2002. See www.prospect. org/cs/articles?article=motor_voter_or_motivated_voter.

200 **"The true test of the American ideal"** Barack Obama, Knox College Commencement address, June 4, 2005, http://en.wikisource.org/wiki/ Commencement_Address%2C_Knox_College_2005.

Index

INDEX

About the Author

Robert Kuttner is founding co-editor of *The American Prospect* and a senior fellow at the think tank Demos. He is author of eight books, most recently *The Squandering of America: How the Failure of Our Politics Undermines Our Prosperity*.

He was a columnist for *Business Week* for twenty years, and continues to contribute columns to the *Boston Globe*. His other writing has appeared in *The New York Times Magazine* and *Book Review*, *The New Yorker*, the *Atlantic*, *Foreign Affairs*, *Harvard Business Review*, *Columbia Journalism Review*, and *Dissent*.

Earlier in his career, he served as a national policy correspondent for *The New England Journal of Medicine*, economics editor of *The New Republic*, a national staff writer and later syndicated columnist for *The Washington Post*, a regular commentator for NPR, and chief investigator of the US Senate Committee on Banking, Housing and Urban Affairs.

He was educated at Oberlin College, the University of California–Berkeley, and the London School of Economics. He has taught at Brandeis, Boston University, the University of Massachusetts, and Harvard's Institute of Politics.

He lives in Boston with his wife, Joan Fitzgerald.

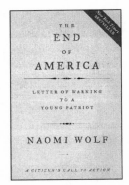
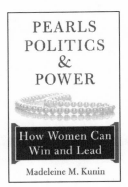

1883755

Made in the USA